Federico García Lorca

Songs

Federico García Lorca

S ONG S

translated by

PHILIP CUMMINGS

With the Assistance of Federico García Lorca

edited by

DANIEL EISENBERG

DUQUESNE UNIVERSITY PRESS, PITTSBURGH

Distributed by Humanities Press, Atlantic Highlands

Publication of this volume was assisted by a grant from the International Poetry Forum.

861.62

Ð16s

100819

apr. 1977

First Printing

Printed in the United States of America

Library of Congress Cataloging in Publication Data

García Lorca, Federico, 1898–1936.
    Songs.

    Translation of Canciones.
    Includes bibliographical references.
    I.   Cummings, Philip H.
PQ6613.A763C313   1976   861'.6'2   75–33155
ISBN 0–391–00414–X

Poesía pura. Poesía impura.
  ("Poema doble del Lago Edem,"
    first version.)

Libro de sorpresa para muchos y de
  alegría para pocos.

  (From a letter to Jorge Guillén.)

CONTENTS

Nocturnes from the Window

Songs for Children

Andalusian Songs

Three Portraits with Shade

Games

Songs of the Moon

Eros with a Stick

The Other World

Plates

[between pages 20 and 21]

[xi]

Cambridge, 20 de noviembre—1974

Mi querido y admirado amigo:

Llegó su gran sobre cuando yo estaba en el hospital de Boston donde había sido operado... Me encuentro ahora, ya en casa, bien, pero bastante cansado.

Pues señor... Es usted un portentoso investigador de Historia Literaria. Ha reunido usted interesantes documentos para ilustrar el capítulo biográfico "Lorca en Nueva York". El posible libro ya tiene un prólogo, que no podría ser superado: las páginas en que usted explica exactamente todo aquel momento americano de Federico. Yo no tengo nada que añadir a ese estudio, inmejorable...

Le agradezco mucho que me haya dado a conocer tales papeles, muy curiosos, ya no ocultos, es decir, perdidos para siempre. ¡Qué ganas tengo de leer el gran volumen "Lorca en Nueva York"! No hay nadie que sepa tanto como usted sobre ese asunto. Gracias una vez más. Y un cordialísimo abrazo de su amigo

Jorge Guillén

EDITOR'S INTRODUCTION

The translation presented here has a unique place in
Lorca scholarship, as it is the only translation of Lorca's
poetry in which the author actively assisted. It was made in
August of 1929 at Eden Mills, Vermont, during the ten days
which Federico spent with his American friend Philip
Cummings after the conclusion of the Columbia University
summer session.[1] According to Cummings, each poem, each
line was discussed with the author, and the result is an
English rendering which reflects Federico's intentions more
faithfully than any other could. The translation is often a
guide to an understanding of the original Spanish.[2]

Philip Cummings[3]

Cummings, whose translation is published here for the
first time, is one of the many colorful and fascinating people
with whom Federico was constantly surrounded. A poet in

[1]See the discussion of dating, below, and the present author's "A
Chronology of Lorca's Visit to New York and Cuba," *Kentucky Romance
Quarterly,* in press.
[2]See "The Poems," p. 183, and p. 14 of this introduction.
[3]The discussion of Cummings and of Lorca's visit to Vermont is based on
Kessel Schwartz, "García Lorca and Vermont," *Hispania,* 42 (1959), 50–55;
"Favorite of Spanish King is Resident of Chapel Hill," *Charlotte* (N.C.)
Observer, June 27, 1937; letters to and from Cummings and miscellaneous
clippings and biographical information in the archives and Alumni Offices
of Rollins College and the University of North Carolina (also see "Pro-
Soviet Bias Charged to Fair," *New York Times,* May 21, 1939, p. 39); con-
versations with Cummings, May 26 and June 20, 1974, and numerous
letters from Cummings to the present writer and to others. I have gone to a

his own right,[4] Cummings was born in 1906 in Hardwick, Vermont, the son of a prosperous insurance and real estate salesman, and after graduation from the Hardwick Academy enrolled in Stetson University in 1924. He interrupted his studies to travel to Europe, first in 1926–27, visiting France and England, and in 1928, after his third and final year at Stetson, to visit Spain. In the summer of 1928 he studied at the University of Madrid, at which time he met Federico and travelled with him to Granada. In Granada he met the Lorca family, and went hiking with Federico in the Sierra Morena and was taken by him to meet some of his friends among the gypsies.

Returning to the United States, Cummings entered Rollins College in 1928, from which school he was to graduate in 1929, receiving *in absentia* the degree of B.A. in Modern Languages. While in Spain in 1928 he had been presented at court, and in a typical gesture he sent the King a copy of his volume *Mother-tongue* upon its publication in December of that year. Cummings conserves as one of his precious possessions a letter of thanks written by the King's secretary, which bears the royal seal.[5] A further result was an invitation from the King to return to Spain to study, and he left in mid-April for Madrid. He was pressed into service assisting in English instruction at the University of Madrid due to the

considerable amount of trouble, more so than might appear, to try to verify from documents the information here presented; one of the various characteristics Cummings shares with Lorca is that he is not overconcerned with the facts of his biography. I have been assisted in this by persons mentioned in the acknowledgements, below.

[4]*Mother-tongue* (Winter Park, Florida: The Rollins Press, 1928), "The One Left Behind" and "Sigüenza," in *American Voices, 1936,* ed. Margaret Nelson (New York: Avon, 1936), p. 92, plus "many verses in Vermont anthologies." He is also the author of *Woodchuck Rampant Bearing Light* (Cleveland: The Rowfant Club, 1944).

[5]Dated January 17, 1929: "By order of His Majesty the King (whom God guard) I give you thanks in his royal name for the volume of poems

academic turmoil created by the political situation. He received among other honors permission to conduct research in the Escorial library, to which he was, however, unable to pay more than a brief visit.[6]

In Spain in 1929 Cummings reaffirmed his invitation to Lorca to visit Vermont, an invitation first made the preceding year. Since Cummings' return to the U.S. in June of 1929 coincided with Federico's sudden decision to visit the United States, the two travelled together as far as Paris, whereupon Cummings went directly to the U.S. and Lorca proceeded to England with Fernando de los Ríos. Cummings was one of the few friends Federico had in the U.S. upon his arrival, and he was one of the first people he turned to for help. Even before he had found, through the intervention of Federico de Onís, lodging in Furnald Hall, a Columbia University dormitory, he wrote to Cummings in Vermont speaking of "esa desesperación de Nueva York," in which, he said, "estoy loco."[7] Cummings telephoned him in New York and sent him money for a train ticket to Vermont, but by that time Federico had enrolled in an English course, in which he was to remain until its conclusion in mid-August.[8]

---

composed by you, which you had the kindness to send, and which has found favor in the sight of the august sovereign. I remain your attentive servant who kisses your hand, Emilio Mano de Torres, El Secretario particular de S. M. El Rey." (Published in translation in the *Charlotte Observer*, June 27, 1937.)

[6]Letter of Cummings to A. J. Hanna, June 7, 1929, in the files of the Rollins College Alumni Association; information card made out in the spring of 1929 in their files.

[7]According to Cummings this letter, together with two others and various autograph poems of Lorca, was stolen from him by a researcher using his papers whom he does not wish to identify. He has understood that they were later sold by a dealer.

[8]See my "Lorca en Nueva York," in *Textos y documentos lorquianos* (Tallahassee, 1975), pp. 17–20.

The letter Lorca wrote to Cummings acknowledging receipt of the money is the only one Cummings still conserves; published by Kessel Schwartz, "García Lorca and Vermont," p. 50, it is still, curiously, missing from Lorca's collected works. Since it is virtually unknown and because it shows clearly the close relationship between the two men, it is reedited here from the original, respecting as much as possible Federico's spelling, accentuation, and punctuation.[9]

> *Querido amiguito mio:*
>
> *Recibi tu carta con gran alegria. He encontrado ya mi sitio en New-York.*
>
> *Deseo verte muy pronto y pienso constantemente en ti pero me he matriculado por consejo de Onis el profesor, en la Universidad de Columbia y yo no puedo por esta causa ir contigo hasta dentro de seis semanas. Si entonces tu sigues queriendo, yo iré a tu lado encantado.*
>
> *Si para entonces tu no estás en tu casa, te ruego vengas a verme a New-York.*
>
> *¿Te parece bien? Escribeme con toda confianza si esto puede ser.*
>
> *Estoy confundido por tu gran amabilidad enviandome el dinero para el billete y desde luego si no se arregla mi viaje*

[9]I have assigned to this undated letter ("Chronology") the date of July 6 or 7, 1929. On it someone in a different ink has underscored "violenta cuidad" and has added at the top of the first page: "¿Conces [sic] Profeso [sic] Fernando de los Rios? Es el jefe de la Univ. de Granada quién ha trovesado [sic] al mar comigo este verano. ¡Que gentil hombre". On the reverse of the first page the same person has added: "Los pobres españoles cuando vienen en Nueva York ¡que diferencia! que ruido ¡que antipatico!" and on the reverse of page two: "Esa es una carta del desteriquido [?] poeta Federico Lorca."

dentro de seis semanas te lo devolveré guardandote siempre
gratitud y lealtad hidalga que es todo lo mejor que puede dar
un español
Escribeme enseguida querido amigo y dime si te parece bien el
retraso de mi viaje. Yo debo hacer, ya que estoy matriculado,
este curso de ingles.
Luego yo pasaria unos dias contigo y serian deliciosos para mi.
Espero que tu me contestarás y no te olvidarás de este poeta del
Sur perdido ahora en esta babilonica cruel y violenta ciudad,
llena por otra parte de gran belleza moderna.
Vivo en Culumbia [sic] y mis señas son estas

> *Mister Federico G. Lorca*
> *Furnald Hall*
> *Columbia University*
> *New-York City*

Espero que tu me contestarás enseguida.
> *Adios queridisimo recibe un abrazo de*
> *Federico.*
Saluda con todo respeto a tus padres.

*　　*　　*

At the conclusion of the Columbia summer session Lorca travelled to Vermont for the memorable visit with Cummings, to which we will return shortly.

Cummings did not see Federico again until 1930, as he spent that academic year teaching French and Spanish at Principia School in St. Louis. But when he returned to Spain in 1930 with a fellowship from the Institute of International Education, he saw much of him, exploring Madrid and visiting the Teatro Español together; at the Teatro Español Lorca introduced him to Margarita Xirgu and Cipriano Rivas Cherif. Among the figures he met was Unamuno, to

[7]

whom Cummings wrote "cold" and whom he visited in Salamanca.[10] But the political events in Spain in the spring of 1931 greatly disturbed Cummings, and he left Spain without finishing his studies.[11]

He was not to see Federico again except for a brief meeting in the summer of 1934. Disheartened, he returned to the United States, travelled in Canada and Mexico, and in the fall of 1931 enrolled in Middlebury College, from whose Department of Spanish he received in 1932 the M.A. degree. In 1932 he began teaching at the Valley Ranch School in Valley, Wyoming, but shortly after his arrival he set out on a round-the-world trip with the son of the owner. On the same boat to Europe was none other than Greta Garbo, with whom he found favor and whose family he visited in Sweden.[12] At the conclusion of the nine-month trip Cummings spent three months on Niue, a Pacific island, living with the natives and studying their language. After

[10]An autograph letter of Unamuno to Cummings, addressed to him at the Fundación del Amo *residencia* in Madrid, is worth preserving:

Sr D^n Felipe Cummings, Madrid

Puede usted venir, señor mio, en cualquiera de los dias que me dice seguro de encontrarme aquí, pues no pienso salir de Salamanca antes de vacaciones de navidad. Las explicaciones que me da de sus propósitos me satisfacen, pues empiezan a molestarme los interviews, *aunque no sean políticos que estos son insoportables. Tendré, pues, gusto en estrechar su mano y más al saber que no escribe más que poesías. Es, por mi parte, hace tiempo que es lo que principalmente escribo.*

Queda suyo afmo

Miguel de Unamuno

Salamanca

11 XI 1930

[11]The *Charlotte Observer* article referred to in n. 2, above, contains a colorful but unfortunately fictitious account of Cummings' association with the royal family and his flight to France with Queen Victoria.

[12]*Charlotte Observer*, June 27, 1937. The year of this trip is established from the discussions of Garbo's trip, *New York Times*, July 31, 1932, p. 23.

two more years at the Valley Ranch School and a trip to Europe in 1934, he enrolled in 1935 in the Department of Romance Languages of the University of North Carolina, intending to obtain a doctorate in Spanish. But although he gave a paper before an AATS meeting in 1936[13] and began a dissertation under the direction of Sturgis Leavitt,[14] he withdrew from that school in 1937, faced with difficulties in obtaining research materials because of the Civil War and discouraged about finding an academic job. Since that time he has made his living primarily as a lecturer and a free-lance economic consultant.

The Visit to Vermont and the Translation of *Canciones*

Es tierra, ¡Dios mío!, tierra, lo que vengo buscando...
Es dolor que se acaba y amor que se consume.
("Tierra y luna," Aug. 28, 1929)

Lorca's visit to Vermont was an essential part of the heal-ing process which was his entire visit to the United States.[15] Whatever he was searching for, he had not found it in New

[13]On the topic "Gustavo Bécquer as Editor of the *Museo Universal,* Madrid 1866" (*Hispania,* 19 [1936], 469).

[14]His topic was "A Glossary of the Academic Editions of Lope de Vega" (UNC Record No. 311, *Research in Progress, October 1935–October 1936* [Chapel Hill: UNC Press, 1936], p. 86). I would like to thank Mr. Michael G. Martin, Jr., Archivist of the University of North Carolina, for finding this information for me.

[15]According to numerous sources, including Federico's own words, shortly before coming to New York he had suffered a serious personal crisis, and he had come to New York to "salir de la penumbra sentimental en que se hallaba" (quoted in González Carbalho, *Vida y muerte de Federico García Lorca* [Santiago de Chile: Ercilla, 1938], p. 30). Although an understanding of this crisis seems essential to an understanding of many poems of *Poeta en*

[9]

York during the summer of 1929. The hot and lonely days
in Furnald Hall, his frustrating English class,[16] the walks

Nueva York, it has been impossible to discover its real nature; the pos-
sibilities are numerous and to a degree contradictory.

According to Cummings, with whom I have gone over line by line Ángel
del Río's comments on Lorca's crisis, and who has read an autobiographical
memoir since destroyed (on which see my *The Textual Tradition of* Poeta en
Nueva York, in press, n. 155), Schonberg's suggestion of a crisis with
Salvador Dalí is incorrect, although Schonberg is correct in discussing
Federico's explosive crisis with his family, of approximately this date. (For
information on Schonberg see "Una visita con Jean-Louis Schonberg," in
Textos y documentos lorquianos, pp. 37–50.) Nevertheless, the letters to Gasch
and Zalamea, whose incorrect ordering has hindered their interpretation
(No. 4 to Zalamea is the earliest of those to him; No. 14 to Gasch is later than
No. 17 and No. 15 is later than Nos. 17–20; No. 20 is earlier than No. 19, in
No. 21 he sends poems he offered to send in No. 22, and No. 16 is the last of
the set), suggest that the crisis came in October of 1928, and up until then
Lorca retained hope that Dalí would come to Granada despite Dalí's evident refusal (see letter No. 22 and then No. 21 to Gasch); it was in October
when Buñuel returned to Spain to attend a film congress and took Dalí to
Paris (see J. Francisco Aranda, *Luis Buñuel, biografía crítica* [Barcelona:
Lumen, 1968], pp. 50 and 58), whereupon the two produced their movie *Le
chien andalou,* which I have suggested in an unpublished article was a satire
on Lorca. According to a well-known professor at Barnard College, the
"chisme de todo Madrid," perhaps no more than that, was that the person
involved was the sculptor Emilio Aladrén, to whom the "Romance del
emplazado" was dedicated and who made a bust of Lorca, photographed in
Social, April 1930, p. 106, yet the chronology of this relationship with
Aladrén, with whom Lorca was also seen after returning to Spain, is
perplexing. Apparently to be ruled out because of date is Federico's
unhappy consideration of marriage (see [Antonio Quevedo], *El Poeta en La
Habana* [(La Habana: Consejo Nacional de Cultura), 1961], p. [13]), and
there is nothing to suggest that Alberti would have caused Federico this
inner turmoil. Both Cummings and the Barnard professor have suggested
that despite the crisis there was a more immediate political reason for
Federico's leaving Spain.

The solution to this question, which I repeat is an important and serious
one, is surely further documents, perhaps his letters from New York to his
mother, recently discovered by the Lorca family, the balance of Morla
Lynch's diary, or his correspondence with Aleixandre and Alberti.

[16]Among others who knew Federico that year I have succeeded in locating
Amy Shaw [Abbott], who taught the English class Federico enrolled in and
who proved a useful source. See "Lorca en Nueva York," pp. 19–20.

with Sofía Megwinoff[17] along Riverside Drive were not the right medicine for his troubled soul, and the opportunity to travel to the Vermont mountains must have seemed to him a chance to escape the uncomfortable city and to commune with a dear friend with whom he shared many interests.

At the time the Cummings family was vacationing at a summer cottage in Eden, Vermont. They received Lorca warmly, travelling to Montpelier Junction to pick him up following his all-night trip from New York City. Cummings and Lorca were constantly together during those days, talking from morning until falling asleep at night, about life, love, and poetry; the two hiked over much of the countryside. Cummings still remembers clearly many memorable moments from Lorca's visit: a rainy morning spent making donuts, with Federico perched on the kitchen stool conversing as best he could with Cummings' mother, an impromptu concert of Spanish folk songs given at the restaurant of the Ruggles family, the "Dew Kum Inn," in which the poems "Cielo vivo" and "Tierra y luna" were written, according to their epigraphs, visits with the Tyler sisters, with whom Federico conversed in French and on whose dilapidated piano he also played, and lying in the grass high in the Vermont mountains during a hike, with much of New England spread before them.

"Una buena experiencia para mí," Federico wrote from

---

[17]Sofía T. Megwinoff [de Lanza], a Puerto Rican of Russian origin whose name was mentioned by Federico in a lecture (incorrectly transcribed, OC, I, 1103). Her thesis, "La poesía de vanguardia en España e Hispanoamérica" (M.A., Columbia, 1930), discusses her meeting with Federico, and also speaks of visiting professor Dámaso Alonso's course at Hunter College and quotes from his then-unpublished book, "La lengua poética de Góngora y su influencia en la literatura contemporánea." She has been kind enough to write me recently some of her recollections of Federico in New York. ("OC" refers to the 18th Aguilar edition of Lorca's works, Madrid, 1973.)

Eden Mills to Ángel del Río.[18] His change in mood, or rather his return to his normally optimistic and happy disposition, is evident from the letters which he wrote to Fernández Almagro and Morla Lynch[19] after his return to New York. Both a result and a cause of his uplifted spirits was his return to creative activity, as he suggests in his letter to Fernández Almagro. He had, by all accounts, virtually stopped writing for a period following his emotional crisis. He had begun writing during the summer, as he brought with him to Vermont a sheaf of partially-completed manuscripts. Yet the experience at Eden Mills allowed him to return to the city in a creative frame of mind, which produced the great burst of activity witnessed by John Crow and Francis Hayes.[20] The poems written in Eden Mills, "Poema doble del Lago Edem,"[21] "Cielo vivo," "Tierra y luna," and others,[22] are at least partly attempts to resolve through poetic expression the inner turmoil he felt.

A lesser-known result of the visit to Eden Mills is the translation of *Canciones* which is published in this volume. At that time Federico's poetry was all but unknown in English.[23] Cummings suggested to Federico translating the

[18]OC, II, 1249.

[19]OC, II, 1115–16 and 1240. If he wrote letters to Spain during the summer these have not been published; these letters suggest that he had let his correspondence slide during the summer, but caught up on it upon his return to New York in the fall.

[20]See John Crow, *Federico García Lorca* (Los Angeles: The Author, 1945), p. 47; also personal communications from John Crow and Francis Hayes, both April 8, 1974.

[21]Lorca consistently spelled "Eden" with an "m"; see *Textual Tradition*, n. 124.

[22]There is some doubt about which of the poems of the section "Introducción a la muerte" of *Poeta en Nueva York* were actually written in Vermont; see *Textual Tradition*, n. 131.

[23]The only published translations at that time were of "Preciosa y el aire" and "Romance de la pena negra," which appeared anonymously in

Romancero gitano, of which some poems had recently been translated into French.[24] Federico challenged him instead to translate *Canciones,* the work which the French translators did not want, the work which, Lorca said, had much more of what was dear to him.[25] The translation was made over the following week, with continuous discussion between Lorca and Cummings over the meaning of the Spanish and the appropriate English equivalents. Cummings himself tells in an earlier introduction how "each poem was a mental wrestling match."[26] Although Federico's English was limited—not nonexistent[27]—he was able to assist Cummings by exegesis in Spanish, which he was under other circumstances always so reluctant to do, or by attention to the phonetics of the English and the syntax and vocabulary as described to him by Cummings.[28] According to Cum-

Alhambra, 1, No. 3 (August, 1929), 25, and the only critical material, aside from the note accompanying these translations, was J. B. Trend's review of *Libro de poemas* in *Alfonso the Sage* (London, 1926), pp. 155–61. (It is not generally known that Trend's review originally appeared in *The Nation and the Athenaeum,* January 14, 1922, pp. 594 and 596.)

[24]This information comes from Cummings; I have been unable to find that this translation had been published at that time. The whole question of translations of Lorca's poetry in the '20's is practically unexplored; Chacón y Calvo mentions a Norwegian translation of this period ("Lorca, poeta tradicional," *Revista de Avance,* No. 45 [April 15, 1930], p. 101); for a Portuguese translation of *Libro de poemas,* see *Textual Tradition,* n. 171.

[25]Lorca's rejection of the *Romancero gitano* and of his association with gypsies by the general public is well known; Martínez Nadal suggests that a cause of his depression was the popularity of this book ("Introduction" to *Poems,* trans. Stephen Spender and J. L. Gili [Oxford Univ. Press, 1939], p. xviii). In his letters to Jorge Guillén in which he speaks of the evolution of *Canciones* as a book, one of its favorable points was that it was not "gitano" (OC, II, 1155).

[26]See "The Poems," p. 183 *infra.*

[27]See "Lorca en Nueva York," p. 20.

[28]"We read all of these poems and argued as to their meanings which I gained very well. He could get the nuances of my translation even if he

mings, these translations stand as approved by Federico.[29]

The English rendering on which the two young men collaborated shows signs of the way it was produced: a tendency to translate line by line, as, for example, in "Little Madrigal," p. 105, and "Echo," p. 106, and reflections of oral transmission of the text from Lorca to Cummings ("sí" is translated "if" in "In the Academy and in the University," p. 104; "qué raro que me llame Federico" is translated with the plural, "From Another Style," p. 115). Perhaps this is why Cummings emphasizes that this is not a polished and revised manuscript and that there are lines in it that he would translate differently today.[30]

Nevertheless, that the translation reflects the discussions of the two men is also evident from the translation itself, and this is, of course, what gives it value as an aid in understanding Federico's original. Particularly important in establishing the translation's claim to authority are the corrections made on it, many when the page was still in the typewriter, without the changes in spacing which are inevitable when a page is removed and later reinserted in the typewriter.[31] Since most of the original translations can be read under the erasures and strikeovers, we have the opportunity to see what the two considered an incorrect translation. For example, in the poem "Suicide," p. 100, the line "Por el balcón se veía una torre" was first translated

---

didn't get the exact words. He liked their sound . . . (letter of Cummings to the present author, July 8, 1974).

[29]P. 183, *infra.*

[30]P. 184, *infra.*

[31]Cummings, a good typist (see Lorca's letter to Ángel del Río, OC, II, 1250), composed these translations at the typewriter; there was no handwritten original. "I pecked [it] out on my father's old Oliver typewriter on the porch of our camp at Eden Lake" (letter to the present author, July 8, 1974).

"From the balcony was seen a tower," a logical translation on the basis of the Spanish alone. The last half of this line was then erased, and it was replaced with "From the balcony he saw himself a tower," a possible translation but not one which would readily occur to an unassisted translator. In "Debussy," p. 67, "privadas de" in l. 4 was first translated "deprived of," then changed to "deprived from." In "Echo," p. 106, "aurora" first became "dawn," then "aurora," and in "Little Madrigal," p. 105, "nuevo" was first translated as "new," then changed to "young."

We thus find that authority is given to the decisions and interpretations that any translator has to make. In "Merry-Go-Round," p. 30, "rabia" is translated as an imperative, whereas in "The Anxiety of the Statue," p. 120, where we can see an attempt to conserve the phonemes of the original, "quita" is not translated as an imperative but rather, with more attention to the sense than the literal meaning, as "it leaves." In "Song of the Dry Orange-Tree," p. 121, "entre espejos" becomes, sensibly, "between" rather than "among mirrors," and "sin toronjas," "without fruitage." At several points there is a suggestion of a textual confusion in the original, corrected by Lorca and Cummings, or perhaps one of Federico's frequent alterations. "Al oído de una muchacha" is translated "To the Hate [odio] of a Girl," surely not an accidental error; the untitled poem "Sobre el cielo verde," p. 111, appears with the new title of "Contrast," and in the sonnet "Long spectre of empassioned silver," p. 112, faced perhaps with problems of rhyme, the two translated "belleza" as "ardor" and "amarilla" as "red."

A constant tendency of this translation is to accentuate the sexual theme of many of these poems. *Doncellas* become "virgins," a *galán* is a lover, *niña* and *muchacha* become "maiden" and *mariquita* is unflinchingly translated as "fairy lad." "Brotando en los dedos," p. 110, appears as "gushing

[15]

out in my fingers." In "Serenade," p. 91, "mueren de amor
los ramos," which Spender and Gili rendered "the flowers
die of love,"[32] Cummings has given us, more suggestively,
"they die of love, the stems." A sexual content to some
poems, such as the sonnet "Long spectre . . . ," "Tree of
Song," and those of "Eros with a Stick," is clear.

Cummings' Diary

Déjame salir hombrecillo de los cuernos
al bosque de los desperezos y los ale-
grísimos saltos . . .
("Poema doble del Lago Edem,"
first version.)

"Perseguido por el licor del romanticismo," Lorca wrote
to Ángel del Río from Eden Mills.[33] The spirit of Lorca's
visit with Cummings is captured in the diary Cummings
kept that August. A Whitmanesque evocation of the landscape and vegetation of this idyllic and unspoiled part of the
United States characterizes the diary from beginning to end.
In it we find a romantic interest in local history and legend,
in ruins, old houses and an abandoned mine, and in the life
of the country people, with an attribution of a mysterious
and even supernatural quality to the surrounding woods
and by extension to all the land.

The editing of this diary has presented several problems.
It reached me incomplete, lacking various interior pages
and the introductory page, with a different title ("Lorca and
Eden"), and somewhat mutilated by earlier editors. With
some effort and Cummings' assistance I have recovered the
missing material and have decided that the conservative

[32]*Poems,* p. 27.
[33]OC, II, 1249.

procedure is to restore it as nearly as possible to its original state. An earlier attempt to abbreviate it, based on what was known of Federico a generation ago, would have removed much that is of interest today.[34]

The reference on p. 159 to the "Spanish poet who has just come" might suggest that only the last part of this diary deals specifically with Federico; nevertheless, someone accompanied Cummings on his hikes in the first part of the diary, as the plural is often used. Upon requesting that Cummings clarify this discrepancy, he wrote as follows: "It was a journal I wrote only to cover the visit of Federico García Lorca.... It started when he came... it ended with his leaving.... If it said recently arrived it would more likely have referred to Frank Ruggles who came up from West Point.... He hiked a few times with us when he was home on leave" (letter to the author, September 30, 1974). It is clear, in any event, that the entire journal reflects the countryside Lorca hiked through with Cummings, the local residents whom he visited with, and above all, the spirit which undoubtedly pervaded his visit.[35]

----

[34]Such as the Tyler sisters, descendants of U.S. President Tyler (not Taylor, as one foreign scholar has mistakenly said). See Schwartz, p. 51, and OC, I, 1101.

[35]A related problem is that of the time period covered by this diary and the date of Federico's visit. The text was divided into 31 numbered divisions, the numbers of which were deleted by Cummings. An identification of the 31 sections with the 31 days of August is, however appealing, impossible for numerous reasons. The introduction to *Canciones* is dated in Hardwick, not Eden, on August 31st; in the final entry of the diary autumn is spoken of as "a month away," which would hardly correspond to August 31. In the eighth section "Saturday" is mentioned, but August 8, 1929, was a Thursday. The first explicit reference to Federico is in the entry 25, yet Lorca dated "Cielo vivo" on August 24th, and Cummings' firm recollection, as also told to Kessel Schwartz (Schwartz, p. 50), Ángel del Río, Mildred Adams, and others, is that Lorca spent ten days in Vermont with him, which is about the right length of time for a translation to be made and for him to

This Edition and Cummings' Introductory Material

The history of this translation and the previous attempts to publish it is a long one, and cannot be discussed here. Several scholars—John Erickson, Kessel Schwartz, Mildred Adams—have worked with this material, with varying amounts of frustration, and Cummings had left instructions for it to be destroyed if it was still unpublished at his death. The most important attempt at publication was that of the Rowfant Club, which considered publication of a selection of the poems and an abridgement of the diary in 1948, and again in 1955, after the publication of Ben Belitt's translation of *Poet in New York*. Cummings wrote introductory material for this projected volume, and it is presented here as the third and final section of this book. Although directed to a general audience, it is of considerable value inasmuch as it is based on first-hand knowledge and evidently not on the limited critical material available at the time, and because it discusses Cummings' acquaintance with Federico and certain ideas, such as his opposition to the Catholic church, which are seldom dealt with.[36]

---

write to Ángel del Río (that he would leave on Thursday, evidently August 29th) after already spending some time with the Cummings family and to receive an answering letter. I have assigned, for these and other reasons, the dates of August 19–August 28 to Federico's visit (see my "Chronology" cited in n. 1).

[36]I am astonished to find that as late as 1966 Lorca's religious ideas are still censored, and that the deleted passages are not restored in the new edition of his works (aside from the fact that we cannot read some poems, such as the "Oda al Santísimo Sacramento," in their entirety). On the deletions in question, from a reading of *Poeta en Nueva York*, see Marie Laffranque, *BHi*, 74 (1972), 556–59. By whom was this censoring done? The whole story of the publication by Editorial Lumen (Barcelona, 1966) of this reading, from a manuscript in the Lorca family archives, is a mystery.

In presenting this material written by Cummings in 1948, as well as his diary, I have corrected spelling in accordance with current usage and have made other minor editorial changes. The translation I have treated with the same respect as one would any text being critically edited, and have not changed even minor aspects without annotating the same. Because the erasures and corrections on the manuscript are of considerable importance, I have noted all but the most minor of them in footnotes.

I would like to thank the many people who have assisted me and made the present volume possible. First, I must give my greatest thanks to Cummings, who entrusted this material to me and who more than anyone else has made me realize the force, charm, and playfulness of Federico's personality. Kessel Schwartz has gone to much trouble in hunting through his records and writing me about his discussions with Cummings in 1957. He, Mildred Adams, and Jorge Guillén read a draft of this introduction and made helpful comments. People at Rollins College, in particular Lynn Paredes Davis and Marilyn F. Boynton of the Alumni Association, and Mrs. Jane Fletcher, Archivist, have gone to the greatest of trouble in poring through old records on my behalf. Mrs. Stella Weston Chapman, Rollins '29, clearly remembers Cummings after 45 years as one of the most remarkable persons she has ever met. At North Carolina I have been helped by Michael G. Martin, Jr., Archivist, Mrs. Monte Roper of the Alumni Association, María Salgado, and Juan Bautista Avalle-Arce; Francis Hayes, Sturgis Leavitt, Albert Engstrom, and Sterling Stoudemire have either told or written me of their recollections of Cummings. Francesca Colecchia of Duquesne University has helped make the publication of this book possible. I have also been assisted by Dr. Theodore

Beardsley, Jr., Director of the Hispanic Society of America, Mrs. Cyrus A. Bunting, Archivist of Principia College, Eugenio Cabrero of the Del Amo Foundation, Carolyn Herr of the Middlebury College Library, Robert Seager of the University of Baltimore, Aurelio M. Espinosa, Jr., James Causey, and last but not least my wife Irene, who assisted me in research in Chapel Hill and patiently accepted the time I have spent researching Cummings and his friendship with Federico.

Tallahassee, Florida
December, 1974

Plates

I Philip Cummings (l.), Cumming's cousin Edna Southwick Stimpson, and Federico García Lorca, in front of an abandoned cabin near Lake Eden.

II Lorca (l.) and Cummings at Lake Eden.

III In front of the "Dew-Kum-Inn." l. to r., first
row, Lorca, Edna Southwick Stimpson, Cummings' mother Mrs. Addie Cummings, and
his aunt, Mrs. Carrie Southwick. Rear, Philip
Cummings.

IV At Lake Eden

V Cummings and Lorca in Eden Mills.

SONGS

Canciones 1921–24

Dedicated to:

Pedro Salinas

Jorge Guillén

and

Melchor Fernández Almagro

INTRODUCTION

One warm afternoon in Madrid I sat on the bench over-looking the city from the Residencia when I was aroused by singing and a music which seemed pregnant with the orange sunshine of Andalusia and to bear the great and melancholy motives of the strange plateaus to the north of Medina del Campo. Looking into the Sala de Conferencias I saw a young, olive-skinned man playing without music, and singing words which moved his distinguished audience of professors.

This was the poet and interpreter of the ever ancient Andalusia, Federico García Lorca. To the foreigner who will at the most only get rare glimpses of the hearts of this tragically sad race, such works as come from the mind and heart of Lorca are priceless intimacies, told with the full-heartedness of intense purpose; the purpose of putting the miracle that is Andalusia before the world in such a way that it will still seem a miracle.

The "Songs" are now in their second edition in Spain, and many have been translated into the major languages of Europe. Even the greatest of translation could not give the true estimate of Lorca's work, for he coins new words when he chooses, he uses words not in the popular vocabulary, and his images are his own. He mentions the black moon and it is black for us. Unrealistic but powerful, rhythm beaten out of new bronze; bronze from the cool hills back of Granada which is the poet's home.

P.H.C.

Hardwick Vermont
August the 31st 1929

[23]

THEORIES

SONG OF THE SEVEN VIRGINS

(Theory of the Rainbow)

They sing, the seven Virgins.
   (Upon the sky a bow of
   the colors of the sunset.)

A soul with seven voices, the seven Virgins.
   (In the white air
   seven large birds.)

They die, the seven Virgins.
   (Why should they not have been nine?
   Why should there not have been twenty?)

The river bears them away,
No more can one see them.

A NOCTURNE BY EQUATION

The fennel, the serpent and the reeds
The fragrance, a trail and glooms;
The air, the earth, and solitude.
   ('Tis a stairway to the moon.)

THE SONG OF THE SCHOOL-BOY

Saturday.
The gate to a garden.
Sunday.
A gray day.
Gray.

Saturday.
Blue clouds.
A breeze.
Sunday.
The sea with shores.
Boundaries.

Saturday.
The seed,
Trembling.
Sunday.
   (Our love is become tawny.)

SONG[1] WISHES TO BE A LIGHT

In the shadow the song has
Threads of phosphorous and moonstuff.
The light does not know what it wishes.
In its opal limits
It finds itself alone
And returns.

[1]The song

[28]

THE MERRY-GO-ROUND

To José Bergamín

Feast days go on wheels.
The Merry-Go-Round carries them
And bears them away.

The blue Body.
A white New Year.

Days cast off their skins
As the serpents
With the sole exception
Of the feast days.

They are even those of our aged mothers.
The afternoons of the long tailed coat
And tinsel.

The blue[1] Body.
A white New Year.

The Merry-Go-Round whirls
Gathered from a star.
A tulip of the five parts
Of the earth.

On little horses
Disguised as panthers,
The children gulp down the moon
As though it were the outside
Of a cherry.[2]

Rage on, rage on[3] Marco Polo!
On a fantastic wheel
Children see
The unknown distances of the earth.

The blue Body.
A white New Year.

[1]All Blue
[2]A cherry.
[3]The fury, the rage of

THE BALANCE

Night is ever quiet.
The day[1] goes and comes.

Night is dead and lofty.
Day is on the wing.

The night is on[2] mirrors,
The day[3] is below the wind.

[1]But the days
[2]Night is beyond all
[3]While the day

SONG WITH MOVEMENT

Yesterday.
    (Blue starlight.)

Tomorrow.
    (Little white stars.)

Today.
    (The dream, the sleeping flower[1]
    in the valley of the petticoat.[2])

Yesterday.
    (Stars of flame.)

Tomorrow.
    (Stars of violet.)

Today.
    (This heart, Oh God,
    this leaping heart!)

Yesterday.
    (Memory of stars.)

Tomorrow.
    (Closed stars.[3])

Today . . .
    (The morrow!)

Perchance I shall be seasick
On the boat?

On the bridges of Today
On the route of the water!

[1]Sleep the flower (then) The sleeping flower of the sex (?)
[2]within the depths of passion.
[3]Stars incomprehensible.

THE PROVERB OF THE SEASON

March
Goes on wing.
January
Follow[s] so haughtily
January, follows
In the nightime of the Heavens.
While March below is
Only a moment.

January.
This for my old eyes.
March.
This for my fresh hands.

FRIEZE

To Gustavo Durán

THE LAND	THE SKY
The little girls of the winds go with their long reins.	The youths of the air leap over the moon.

THE HUNTER

High Pine-grove!
Four doves which go through the air.

Four doves
Which return and turn.
They bear wounds
By their shadows.

Lowly Pine-grove!
Four doves
Lie on the earth.

FABLE

Unicorns and Cyclops.

Horns of gold
And eyes of green.

On the lofty promontories
Is the gigantic mob
Without glass
In the quicksilver of the sea.

Unicorns and Cyclops.

One pupil and one power.

Who doubts the sureness,
The terror of these horns?

You hide your bulls-eyes,
O Universe!

August
The counterpart
Of peach and sugar-cane
And the sun of afternoon
As the pit within a fleshy fruit.

The corn husks[1] still holds intact
Its hard and yellow smile.

August
While the children eat
Black bread and the richest Moon.

[1]stalk

HARLEQUIN

The red breast of the sun.
The blue breast of the moon.
Middle trunk of coral
A half body of
Silver and of shade.

THREE TREES WERE CUT

To Ernesto Halffter

They were three.
(The day came with its axes.)
They were two.
(Low wings of silver.)
There was one.
There was none.
(The water was left
In Nudity.)

NOCTURNES FROM THE WINDOW

To the memory of José de Ciria y Escalante
Poet.

1.

High goes the moon.
Low rushes the wind.
   (My distant gazes
   search the sky.)

Moon on the waters.
Moon below the wind.
   (My nearer gazes
   search the earth.)

The voices of two little girls.
Without courage I went
From the moon on the water
To the moon in the sky.

2.

One arm of the night
Comes through my window.

A great dark arm
Which pulses with water.

On a blue crystal
My soul plays at the river.

The moments wounded by
The clock . . . pass away.[1]

[1]pass by.

3.

I lean my head from the window
And I see, as though it wished
To cut it off, the keen knife
Of the wind.

In this invisible guillotine
Have I placed
All the sightless heads
Of my desires.

And an[1] odor of lemon
Fills this immemorable moment
Meanwhile the wind
Is become a flower of tulle.

[1]The

4.

At the pool has been killed
Today a little child of the water.
She was outside the pool
On the enshrouded earth.

From the top of her thighs
Crosses a fish, calling her.
The wind says "little child"
But they can not rouse her.

The pool has loosened
The long hair of the sea-weed
And to the air its grey bosom
Quivering with frogs.

God saves you. Let us pray
To Our Lady of the Waters
For the maiden of the pool
Who died under the apple boughs.

I then will place at your side
Two small calabashes
To keep you afloat,
Ah,[1] on the briny sea.

RESIDENCIA DE ESTUDIANTES 1923

[1]You

SONGS FOR CHILDREN

To the remarkable child
Columba Morla Vicuña
who died the 12th of August 1928

SONG OF CHINA IN EUROPE

To my god-child Isabel Clara

The lady with the fan
Goes over the bridge
Of the cool river.

The gentlemen in their frock-coats,
Look at the bridge
Without balustrades.

The lady of the fan
And of veils
Looks for a spouse.

The gentlemen are married
To the tall[1] blonds
Of the pale language.

The crickets chirp in the west.
   (The lady passes over the greensward.)

The crickets chirp beneath the flowers.
   (The gentlemen go toward the north.)

[1]haughty

[45]

LITTLE SONG OF SEVILLE

To Solita Salinas

Dawn in the orange groves
Golden bees gathering honey.

Where will the honey be?

'Tis in the blue flower,
Isabel.
In the flower
Of the rosemary.

A small gold seat
For the moor,
A chair of gilt
For his lady.

Dawn
In the orange grove.

THE SNAIL SHELL

To Natalita Jiménez

They have brought me a snail shell.

Within it sings a sea of[1] a map.
My heart
Fills with its water,
With small fishes
Of shadows,
And of silver.

They have brought me a snail shell.

[1]from

To Mademoiselle Teresita Guillén
playing her little piano of six keys.

The lizard is weeping.
His mate is weeping.

The lizard and his mate
With little white aprons
Have lost, without intention
Their nuptial rings.

Ah, their little ring of lead!
Ah their weighted ring!

A great heaven and without people
Rises as a globe to the birds.

The sun, the circled captain
Wears a vest of satin.

Look at them, how old they are!
How old are the lizards!

Ah, how they weep and weep,
Ah, ah, how they are weeping!

A CHANTED SONG

In the gloaming
The Griffon bird
Cloathes itself in grey.[1]
And the little girl Kikirikí
Has lost her paleness
Has lost her form, there.

To enter into the gloaming
I painted myself with gloamy grey,
And how I, myself have shone
In the gloom.

[1]gloom.

LANDSCAPE

To Rita, Concha, Pepe and Carmencica.

The erring afternoon
Garbed itself in frost.

Behind the dim panes
All the children
See changed into birds
A yellow tree.

The afternoon is drawn out
As the length of the river.
And a red ball of an apple
Quivering over the little tiled roofs.

[49]

SILLY SONG

Mama
I would be silver.
My son
You would be very cold.

Mama
I would be of water.
My son
You would be very cold.

Mama
Tuck me into your pillow.

That, oh yes!
And even now.

ANDALUSIAN SONGS

To Miguel Pizarro
(in the symmetrical irregularity of Japan.)

SONG OF THE CAVALIER
(1860)

In the black moon-cloud
Of the bandits,
Chant the spurs.

    Black little nag
    Where do you bear your dead cavalier?

. . .The harsh spurs
Of the motionless bandit
Who has lost the reins.

    Cold little nag
    What perfume bears the flower of the dagger!

In the black moon-cloud
The sides of the Sierra Morena
Are bathed in blood.

    Black little nag
    Where do you bear your dead cavalier?

The night spurs
Its black loins
Riveting itself in stars.

    Cold little nag
    What perfume bears the flower of the dagger!

In the black moon-cloud
A scream!

[53]

And the long spiral
Of the bonfire.

    Black little[1] nag
    Where do you bear your dead cavalier?

[1]Little black

ADELINA ON A WALK

The sea has no oranges
Nor has Seville any of love.
Dark, what light is of the fire.
Lend me your parasol.

I will put on the green face
—of the essence of lime and lemon—
Your words—little fishes—
Which will swim around and around.

The sea has no oranges.
Ah love.[1]
Seville has none of love!

[1]And love?

[54]

Blackberry with the grey trunk,
Give me a branch for myself.

Blood and thorns, I approach you.
If you love me, I will love you.

Leave your fruit of green and shadow
On my tongue, blackberry.

What a long embrace I have given you
In the shade of my thorns!

Blackberry, where dost thou go?
To seek loves which you do not give me.

My maiden has gone to sea
To count the waves and tiny white pebbles,
But she found herself suddenly
With the river of Seville.

Among oleanders and church spires
Five boats sail along
With oars dipped in the water
And sails spread to the breeze.

Who looks within the
Tower harnessed as a mule of Seville[1]?
Five voices answered
Rounded as little rings.

[55]

The sky rises gracefully
To the river, from shore to shore.
In the reddened air
Five rings waver.

¹Adorned tower of Seville

THE AFTERNOON

(Was it my little Lucía wading in the brook?)

The giant poplars
And a star.

The silence cut
By the frogs, seeming
As a painted tulle
With little green moons.

In the river
A withered tree
Which has flowered
In concentric circles.

And I have dreamed
On the waters
Of a little dark child
Of Granada.

THE SONG OF THE HORSEMAN

Cordoba
Distant and alone.

Black mare, big moon
And little olives in my saddle-bags.
Even if she knows the road
Never shall I arrive at Cordoba.

Over the plain, through the wind
Black mare, red moon.
Death is looking at me
From the towers of Cordoba.

Oh how long the road!
Oh how courageous my horse!
Oh the death that awaits me
Before I arrive at Cordoba!

Cordoba
Distant and alone.

IT IS TRUE

Oh what pain it costs me
To love you as I love you!

By your love the very air wearies me
My heart
Even my hat.

Who would buy me, even me
The ring which I have
And this sadness of white linen
To be used for handkerchiefs.

Oh what pain it costs me
To love you as I love you!

Aged tree, aged tree[1]
Of dried verdancy.

The maiden with the lovely face
Is gathering ripe olives.
The wind, lover of towers
Takes her around the waist.
Four horsemen pass
On Andalusian steeds
With suits of blue and green
With large, obscure capes.
    "Come to Cordoba, maiden!"
The child does not heed[2] them.
There pass three young toreros
Full chested from the waist[3]
With clothing orange color,
And swords of ancient silver.
    "Come to Seville, maiden!"
The child does not heed[2] them.
When the evening is turned violet
With a light diffused;
There passes a youth
Who bears roses
And myrtle of the moon.
    "Come to Granada, maiden."
She does not heed[2] him.
The maiden with the lovely face
Continues gathering ripe olives,
With the grey arms of the wind
Around her waist.

Aged tree, aged tree
Of dried verdancy!

[1]Aged trees, aged trees
[2]listen to
[3]Level . . . d from their waists

Lover
Little lover
In your house burns wild thyme.

That you never go, that you never come
With a key I lock the door.

With a key of fine silver
A key tied with a ribbon.

In the ribbon is an inscription:
"My heart is far away."

Do not return to my street
Leave it all to the open air.

Lover
Little lover
In your house burns the wild thyme.

THREE PORTRAITS WITH SHADE

VERLAINE

The song
that I never shall utter,
has slept on my lips.
The song,
that I never shall utter.

Upon the honeysuckles
was poised a glow-worm
and the moon pecked
with a ray into the water.

Then I dreamed
the song
that I shall never utter.

Song full of lips
and of distant little canals.

Song full of hours
lost in the shade

Song of a living star
above[1] a perpetual day.

[1]over

BACCHUS

Green untouched murmuring.
The fig-tree stretches its arms to me.

[63]

As a panther its shadow
waylays my lyric shadow.

The moon counts the dogs.
It makes a mistake and begins again.

Yesterday, tomorrow, black and green
you circle my brow with laurels.

Who would love you as I
if you should quit your heart of me[1]?

... And the fig-tree cries out to me and advances
terrible and multiplied.

[1]change your heart toward me

JUAN RAMÓN JIMÉNEZ

In the infinite white
snow, spikenard and salt[1]
he lost his fantasy.

The white color, goes
on a silent carpet
of the wings of a dove.

Without eyes or gesture
immovable it suffers a dream.
But trembles within.

In the infinite white,
what pure and long wound
your fantasy has left!

In the infinite white.
Snow.
      Spikenard.
            Salt.

[1]salt of the sea

VENUS

Thus I saw you.

The young dead woman[1]
in the shell of the bed,
stripped of flower and zephyr
emerged the eternal light.

[65]

The world that was left
lily of cotton and shadow,
appeared at the panes
seeing the infinite transition.

The young dead woman,
cleft love from within.
In the foam of the sheets
was[2] lost her tresses.

[1]The young woman
[2]she

DEBUSSY

My shadow goes silently
upon[1] the water of the shallows.

By my shadow are the frogs
deprived from[2] the stars.

The shadow sends to my body
reflections of quiet things.

My shadow goes as an immense
gnat of violet color.

A hundred crickets wish to gild
the light of the reeds.

A light is born in my breast
reflected by the shallows.

[1]through
[2]of

NARCISSUS

Lad.
Are[1] you going to fall into the river!

    In the depth there is a rose
    and in the rose another river.

See that bird!

[67]

Look at the yellow bird!

My eyes are cast
into the water.

My God!
How you slide[2]! Boy!

... and in the rose am I myself.

When he was lost in the water
I understood. But I do not explain.

[1]Do
[2]sink

GAMES

Dedicated to the head of Luis Buñuel
En gros Plan

RIVER SONGS

(With accompaniment of the bells.)

They say that you have a face
(Balalín)
of the full moon.
(balalán)
How many bells do you hear?
(balalín)
They do not leave me.
   (Balalán!)
But your eyes ... ah!
(balalín)
... pardon, your blue eye shadows ...
(balalán)
and that[1] smile of gold
(balalín)
and that ... I can not, that ...
(balalán)

Their stiff crinoline skirt
the bells shake out.

Oh, you enchanting secret! .. you ...
(balalín
lín
lín
lín ...)

Forgive.

[1]this

[71]

TO IRENE GARCÍA

(maid)

In the grove
the young poplars dance
one with the other.
And the old tree,
with its four saplings
dances also.

Irene!
Then will come the rains
and the snows.
You dance on the green.

On the green green,
and I will accompany you.

Ah how runs the water!
Ah my heart!

In the grove
the young poplars dance
one with the other.
And the old tree,
with its four saplings
dances also.

[72]

TO THE HATE OF A GIRL

I do not wish.
I do not wish to say anything to you.

I saw in your eyes
two little crazy trees.
Of breeze, of laughter and of gold.

They moved about.

I do not wish.
I do not wish to say anything to you.

PEOPLE AND AUTUMN

The people went
and the autumn came.

The people
went to the green.
They carried cocks
and happy guitars.
Through the reign
of the seedlings.
The river dreamed,
the fountain ran.
Leap,
hot heart!

The people
went[1] to the green.

The autumn came[2]
yellow of star,
sickened birds
and concentric waves.
On the stiff fronted breast,
the head.
Stop,
heart of wax!

The people went
and the autumn came.

[1]go
[2]comes

THE SONG OF THE FAIRY LAD

The fairy lad combs his hair
in his robe of silk.

The neighbors smile
in their highest windows.

The fairy lad arranges
the curls on his head.

Through the patios call parrots,
fountains and planets.

The fairy lad adorns himself
with a shameless jasmine.

The afternoon becomes beyond
combs and climbing weeds.

The scandal was trembling
striped as a zebra.

The fairy lads of the South
sing on the flat roof-tops!

TREE OF SONG

For Ana María Dalí

The cane of voice and gesture,
one time and another
trembles without hope
in the air of yesterday.

The maiden sighing
wished to gather it;
but always arrived
a minute afterwards.

Ah sun! Ah, moon, moon!
A minute afterwards.
Sixty grey flowers
entangled her feet.

See how they stir themselves
one time and another,
virgin of flower and branch,
in the air of yesterday.

Orange and lemon.

Ah the maiden
of evil love!

Lemon and orange.

Ah the maiden
of the white maiden!

Lemon.

(How shines the sun.)

Orange.

(In the white pebbles of the water.)

THE STREET OF THE DUMB

Behind the immovable panes
the girls play with their smiles.

(In the empty piano,
spider puppet players.)

The girls speak with their lovers
shaking their compressed braids.

(World of the fan,
the handkerchief and the hand.)

The lovers reply making,
wings and flowers with their black capes.

SONGS OF THE MOON

To José F. Montesinos

THE MOON COMES OUT

When the moon goes out
the bells are lost
and the paths appear
impenetrable.

When the moon goes out
the sea covers the earth
and the heart feels itself
an island in infinity.

Nobody eats oranges
under the full moon.
It is necessary[1] to eat
green and frosty fruit.

When the moon goes out
with a hundred equal faces
the money of silver
sobs in the pockets.

[1]delightful

TWO MOONS OF THE AFTERNOON

1

(To Laurita, friend of my sister.)

The moon is dead, dead;
but will live again in the spring.

[81]

When in front of the willows
the south wind whirls.

When our hearts give
their harvest of sighs.

When the thatched roofs
put on their little caps of grass.

The moon is dead, dead;
but will live again in the spring.

2

(To Isabelita, my sister.)

The afternoon sings
a "berceuse" to the oranges.

My little sister sings:
"The earth is an orange."

The moon weeping, says:
"I wish to be an orange."

It can not be, my daughter,
even though you wear rose.
Nor even a small lemon!
What a pity!

MONDAY, WEDNESDAY, AND FRIDAY

I was.
I have been.
But I am not.

I was . . .
(Oh marvelous throat
that of the cypress and its shadow!
Angle of full moon.
Angle of lonely moon.)

I have been . . .
The moon was from the mist
saying that it was a rose.
(With a cape of wind
my love flung itself to the waves.)

But I am not . . .
(Before a broken window
I sew my lyric web.)

SHE DIED AT DAWN

Night of four moons
and of one solitary tree,
with one solitary shadow
and one solitary bird.

I seek in my flesh
marks of your lips.
The spring kisses the wind
without touching it.

I bear the No that you said to me
in the palm of my hand,
as a lemon of wax
almost white.

Night of four moons
and a solitary tree.
On the point of a needle
is my love spinning!

THE FIRST ANNIVERSARY

The maiden passes in front of me.
Oh what an ancient grief!

Of what use to me, I ask
is the ink, the paper and the verse?

Your flesh appears to me
a red lily, a fresh reed.

Darkness of the black moon.
What do you wish of my desires?

[84]

THE SECOND ANNIVERSARY

The moon fastens in the sea
a large horn of light.

Unicorn grey and green,
quivering but overpowering.

The sky floats in the air
as an immense lotus flower.

(Oh you alone treading[1]
the last watch of the night!)

[1]passing

FLOWER

To Colin Hackforth

The magnificent willow
of the rain, falls.

Oh the round moon
on the white branches!

EROS WITH A STICK

(1925)

To Pepín Bello

FRIGHT IN THE DINING ROOM

You were rose.
You became wan lemon.

What design did you see in my hand
that almost threatens you?

I wished green apples.
Not rosy apples . . .

wan lemon . . .

(Crane asleep in the afternoon,
placed on the earth the other foot.)

LUCÍA MARTÍNEZ

Lucía Martínez
Shady spot of red silk.

Your thighs as the afternoon
go from the light to the shade.
The concealed jet
hides your magnolias.

Here I am, Lucía Martínez.
I go to exhaust your mouth
and to drag you by the hair
in the dawn of shells.

Because I wish, and because I can.
Shady spot of red silk.

THE MAIDEN LADY AT MASS

Under the Moses of the incense,
she sleeps.

Eyes of the bull looked[1] at you.
Your rosary rained.[2]

With that dress of deep silk,
you do not move, Virginia.

Give the black melons of your breasts
to the murmur of the mass.

[1]looks
[2]rains

INTERIOR

I do not wish to be a poet,
nor gallant.

White sheets where you are dismayed!

You do not know the dream
nor the splendor of the day.
As the squids,
you blind naked in perfumed ink.
Carmen.

NU

Under the oleander without moonlight
you were ugly[1] nude.

Your flesh sought in my map
the yellow of Spain.

How ugly you were, French lassie
in the bitterness of the oleander.

Red and green, I threw to your body
the cape of my talent.

Green and red, red and green.
Here we are other people!

[1]are horrid

SERENADE

(Homage to Lope de Vega)

Along the banks of the river
the very night is dripping
and in the breasts of Lolita
they die[1] of love, the stems.

They die of love, the stems.

The naked night sings
upon the bridges of March.
Lolita laves her body
with briny water and spikenards.

They die of love, the stems.

The night of anise and silver
shines on the roof-tops.
Silver of brooks and mirrors.
Anise of thy white thighs.

They die of love, the stems.

[1]live

IN MÁLAGA

Sumptuous Leonarda.
Pontifical flesh and white robe,
on the balustrades of the "Villa Leonarda."
Displayed to the trams[1] and boats.
Black bathing[2] bodies hide
the shore of the sea. Swaying
—shell and lotus at a time—
comes your hips
of Ceres in rhetoric of marble.

[1]trolleys
[2]Black bodies

THE OTHER WORLD

To Manuel Ángeles Ortiz

SCENE

High towers.
Long rivers.

FAIRY

Take the marriage ring
that you[r] grandfathers bear it.
One hundred hands, below the earth,
Are finding fault[1] with it.

I

I go to feel in my hands
a great flower of fingers
and the symbol of the ring.
I do not want it.

High towers.
Long rivers.

[1]Find fault

UNEASINESS AND NIGHT

Bee-eater.
In your obscure trees.
Night of stuttering sky
and stammering air.

Three drunkards perpetuate
their expressions of wine and sadness.
The stars of lead revolve
upon a foot.

Bee-eater.
In your obscure trees.

Ache[1] of the temples oppressed
with the wreath of minutes.
And your silence? The three
drunkards sing naked.[2]
Cross-stitch of pure silk
your song.

    Bee-eater.
Eater eater eater eater.
    Bee-eater.

[1]Sorrow
[2]drunkards naked.

THE DUMB YOUTH

The youth seeks his voice.
(The king of the crickets has it.)
In a drop of water
The youth sought his voice.

I do not wish it to speak with;
I will make with it a ring
which my silence will bear
on its little finger.

In a drop of water
the youth sought his voice.

(The captive voice, far away
put on the robe of a cricket.)

THE CRAZY BOY

I said, "Afternoon."
But it was not so.
The afternoon was another thing
and already had passed on.

(And the light contracts
its shoulders as a maiden.)

"Afternoon." But it is useless!
This is false, this has
half a moon of lead.
The other will never come.

(And the light as all see it
was playing at the statue with a crazy boy.)

That[1] was small
and ate pomegranates.
This is huge and green, I can not
take it in my arms nor dress it.
It will not come? How was it?

(And the light that it might go, made a jest.
It separated the crazy boy[2] from his shadow.)

[1]It
[2]child

MARRIAGE-VOW

Throw this ring
to the water.

(The shade puts its fingers
on my shoulder.)

Throw away this ring. I have
more than a hundred years. Silence!

Ask me nothing!

Throw this ring
to the water.

THE LEAVE-TAKING

If I die
leave the balcony open.

The boy eats oranges.
(From my balcony I see it.)

The reaper cuts the wheat.
(From my balcony I feel it.)

If I die,
leave the balcony open!

SUICIDE

(Perhaps it was because you did not know the geometry.)

The small lad forgot[1] himself.
It[2] was at ten in the morning.

His heart was filling itself
of broken wings and tattered flowers.

He noticed that it did not leave him
More than one word in his mouth.

And at leaving his gloves, it fell
from his hands, soft ashes.

From the balcony he saw himself a tower.[3]
He felt himself balcony and tower.

He saw, without doubt, as he looked at it
the clock held in his place.

He saw his shadow long[4] and still,
in the white divan of silk.

And the rigid youth, geometric
with an axe broke the mirror.

On breaking it, a great gush of shadow
flooded the chimerical[5] bedroom.

[1]forget [Editor's alteration.]
[2]They
[3]was seen a tower.
[4]distent
[5]fantastic

LOVE

(With wings and arrows)

LITTLE SONG OF THE FIRST DESIRE

In the green morning
I wished to be a heart.
A heart.

And in the ripe afternoon
I wished to be a nightingale.
A nightingale.

(Soul, put on orange color.
Soul, put on orange color.)

In the living morning
I wished to be I.
A heart.

And in the waning afternoon
I wished to be my voice.
A nightingale.

(Soul, put on orange color,
Soul, put on orange color!)

The first time
I did not know you.
The second, yes.

Tell me if the air tells you.
The small cool morning
I became sad
and then there entered me
desires to laugh.
I did not know you.
If you knew me.
If I knew you
You did not know me.
Now among the two
is stretched impassibly
a month, as a folding[1]
screen of gray days.

The first time
I did not know you.
The second, yes.

[1]"Folding" added in pen.

LITTLE MADRIGAL

Four pomegranates
has your orchard.

(Take my young[1] heart.)

Four cypresses
will have your orchard.

(Take my old heart.)

Sun and moon.
then . . .
neither heart
nor orchard!

[1]new

ECHO

Already has opened
the flower of the aurora.[1]

(Do you remember,
the depth of the afternoon?)

The spikenard of the moon
sends out its cold odor.

(Do you remember
the look of August?)

[1]dawn

IDYL

To Enrique Durán

You wished that I should tell you
the secret of the spring.

I am for the secret
the same as the silver-tree.

Tree whose thousand little fingers
pointing out a thousand little roadways.

Never will I tell you, my love,
because slowly runs the river.

But I will place in my sealed voice
the watery reflection of your look.

Turn around me, little black one!
Have care of my tiny leaves.

Turn[1] more around me
playing at the water-wheel of love.

Ah! I cannot tell you, even should you wish
the secret of the spring.

[1]Give

[107]

NARCISSUS

Narcissus.
Your odor.
And the depth of the river.

I wish to leave myself at your rim.
Flower of love.
Narcissus.

Through you[r][1] white eyes cross
waves and sleeping fishes.
Birds and butterflies
japanize in my eyes.

You diminutive and I great.
Flower of love.
Narcissus.

The frogs, how ready they are!
But I do not leave quiet
the mirror in which is seen
your delirium and my delirium.

Narcissus.
My sorrow.
Even my sorrow.

[1]For your

GRANADA AND 1850

From my room
I hear the fountain.

A finger of the vine
and a ray of sun,
point out towards the spot
of my heart.

Through the air of August
go the clouds. I,
dream that I do not dream
within the fountain.

PRELUDE

The poplar groves go away
but leave us their reflection.

The poplar groves go away
but they leave us the wind.

The wind is enshrouded[1]
at length beneath the sky.

But it has left floating
upon the rivers, its echoes.

The world of the glow-worms
has entered my memories.

And a tiny heart
goes gushing out in my fingers.

[1]enshrined

CONTRAST

On the green sky
a green evening star,
What have you to do, love,
ah, if you do not love yourself?

The towers melted
with cold fog,
how have they to look at us
with their little windows?

One hundred green evening stars
on a green sky,
they do not see a hundred towers
of white, in the snow.

And this anguish of mine
in order to make it live,
I have to decorate it
with red smiles.

SONNET

Long spectre of empassioned silver
the cool wind of the long night with sighing
has opened with grey hand my aged sliver
and then it leaves: I who was desiring.

Wound of love which will even give me life
perpetual blood and purely gushing light.
Cleft in which Philomel voices no strife
will have a wood, pain and a softer height.

Ah, what sweet murmur have I in my head!
I will stretch it to a simple flower
where floats without a soul your ardor.

And the wandering water will come red
while runs my blood deep within the bower
wet and fragrant to its very border.

SONGS FOR THE ENDING

To Rafael Alberti

FROM ANOTHER STYLE

The bonfire pierces the field of the afternoon
some horns as of an enraged deer.
The valley stretches itself out. Through its ridges
wheels the little wind.

The air crystalizes under the vapour.
—Eye of a sad and yellow cat—.
I in my eyes idle among the branches.
The branches tread over the river.

My essential things arrive.
They are phrases of phrases.
Among the reeds of the waning afternoon,
how rare that they should call me Federico!

SONG OF NOVEMBER AND APRIL

The cloudy sky
draws my white eyes.

I to give them life
gather to them a yellow flower.

Not with oneself to disturb them.
They proceed rigid and white.

(Between my shoulders flies
my golden and full soul.)

[115]

The sky of April
draws my eyes of indigo.

I, in order to give them a soul
fasten to them a white rose.

Not by itself to fuse
the white into the indigo.

(Between my shoulders flies
my impassible and blind soul.)

Water, where do you go?

Laughing I go over the river
to the shores of the sea.

Sea, where do you go?

I go seeking the upper river
a fountain wherein to rest.

Willow, and you, what will you do?

I do not wish to tell you anything.
I . . . to tremble!

What I desire, what I do not wish,
over the river, and over the sea?

(Four birds without direction
Are in the tall willow.)

[116]

THE DECEITFUL MIRROR

Green branch free
of rhythm and of bird.

Echo of a sob
without pain or lip.
Man and the Forest.

I weep in front of the bitter sea.
There are in my pupils
two singing seas[1]!

[1] two singing (handwritten change)

USELESS SONG

Future rose and temperate vein,
amethyst of yesterday and breeze of this hour,
I wish to forget them!

Man and fish in their environs, under floating things,
waiting in the seaweed or in a chair the night,
I wish to forget them!

I
Only I!
Working a tray
on which my head will not be placed.
I alone!

[117]

THE ORCHARD OF MARCH

My appletree,
has already shade and birds.

What a leap my dream gives
from the moon to the wind.

My appletree
already gives its arms to the green.

Since March, how I see
the white face of January!

My appletree . . .
(lowly wind).

My appletree . . .
(lofty sky).

TWO SAILORS ON THE SHORE

To Joaquín Amigo

1st

There is borne in the heart
a fish of the Chinese Sea.

At times it is seen to cross
tiny, before his[1] eyes.

Being a sailor he forgets
saloons[2] and oranges.

He looks at the water.

2nd

He had the tongue of soap.
He washed his words and was still.

Level earth and curly sea,
a hundred stars and his boat.

He sees the balconies of the Pope
and the gilded breast of the Cuban women.

He looks at[3] the water.

[1]your (handwritten change)
[2]the saloons (handwritten change)
[3]in (handwritten change)

THE ANXIETY OF THE STATUE

Murmur.
Even though nothing be left than the murmur.

Aroma.
Even though nothing be left than the aroma.

But it wrenches from me the memory
and the color of the ancient hours.

Dolour.
In front of magic and living dolour.

[Battle.]
In actual and unclean battle.

But it leaves the invisible people
that forever surround[1] my house!

[1]surround forever (handwritten change)

SONG OF THE DRY ORANGE-TREE

To Carmen Morales.

Woodman.
Cut for me the shades.
Free me from the martyrdom
of seeing myself without fruitage.

Why was I born between mirrors?
Day reflects me
and the night copies me
in all its stars.

I wish to live without seeing myself.
And ants and downy seeds,
I will dream that these[1] are my
leaves and my birds.

Woodman.
Cut for me the shades.
Free me from[2] the martyrdom
of seeing myself without fruitage.

[1]they (handwritten change)
[2]of (handwritten change)

SONG OF THE DAY WHICH WANES

What toil it costs me
to let you depart, day!
You go filled with me,
you return without knowing me.
What pain it costs me
to leave on your breast
possible realities
of impossible minutes.

In the afternoon, a Perseus
polishes for you the chains,
and you fly over the mountains
wounding your feet.
My flesh nor my weeping
can seduce you,
nor the rivers in which you sleep out
your golden siesta.

From Orient to Occident
I bear your encircled light.
Your great light which sustains
my soul, in sharp tension.
From Orient to Occident
what pain[1] it costs me
to bear you with your birds
and with you[r] arms of the wind.

[1]toil

[122]

The following poem was translated after Federico's death by the New Englander, with special regard as it was written at Eden Lake and is one of the poems of the group *Introduction to Death, Poems of Solitude in Vermont* [of *Poet in New York*], and dedicated to Rafael Sánchez Ventura. [Translator's Note]

RUIN

Alone
I travelled beyond the whiteness
Of my dormant body,
Even thus I travelled the air.
Soon I learned
The moon was a horse's skull
and the air the inside of
A dusky shadowy apple.
Beyond the lattices and lights
Of the window was heard
The ageless struggle of
Sand with the water.
I saw the birth of the grasses
And placed a lamb to graze upon them
A lamb that bleated through its
Tiny mouth, pranced on its tiny hooflets.
There within one drop of dew
The leaden and transparent eggshell
Of the first dove of morning.
The cloud[1] ranges in flocks
Remained still and asleep as I
Saw the eternal battle of rocks with
Day's breaking.

So comes the grass, oh son,
Already there sounds the clash of
Its spears of dampness through
The empty heavens.
My hand, my hand, oh Love. The grasses . . .
The sedges . . .
Through the broken panes
Blood let flow its tresses
Within the house.
You, You alone with me remain here.
Go prepare your skeleton too for the air
You, you alone with me remain here.
Go prepare your form for forever
You must hurry, hurry, hurry,
To attain our shape and no
Dreaming.

[1]Clouds [Editor's Alteration]

August in Eden

An Hour of Youth

by

Philip H. Cummings

1929

FOREWORD

Eden really exists in the low worn-down hills of New England. It is even politically known as Eden and might very well be known as such to those who have wandered along its winding hill roads. We, being a happy family, in the ordinary sense of the word, spent one glorious August in Eden.

The Boy felt that Eden was too charming to live for one August alone. He wished other people to know what summering in Eden can mean so he wrote what each day did to him. It isn't literary but could be called pastoral. It is a prosy appreciation of the great open poem of the woods and lakes of Eden.

P.H.C.

The Principia
September 15th 1929

The stars have gathered in the spaces where the deeply-clasped storm clouds have broken. The lake has been lulled to a pure mirror-like placidity and the long files of hills and trees have been doubled inversely in the multiplication of the dusky hours. The solitary ghost-shadow of a low skimming bat moves over the clear reflection on the lake of the evening sky—a thing of patched clouds and sociable stars.

The only sound is a soft gurgling trickle as the oars cut the cool surface, and voices pass across the silent surfaces as though in awe of the whole situation. We are all as worshipers at the vesper service of a great cathedral. Our one nave is studded with the distant votaries and the taut quiet is a sympathetic medium for full prayer. It is not in what we say, but rather in the intensity with which we feel.

The lake was rough-shod this afternoon and the gusts of wind swept in on us, lying beside a big log, and trying to understand the infinite beauty of Whitman. Where better could we enter into a familiar companionship with this great Interpreter than in the outdoors of a mountain landscape? The storm clouds and the wind movement gave a scenic background, making a living vitaphone of the words of our great Walt.

We are all so prone to discuss the work of the day, the sunset, the storm—everything which has particularly moved us, in the terms: "If I could only put that on paper!" Whitman has put it all down for all of us. He has grasped a whole humanity and made significant gestures at those forbidden subjects which we usually cast aside as "quite beyond us"—a sort of mental shrugging of the shoulders on our part. Nothing seems to have been beyond the pen of Walt Whitman, though he may only have touched some subjects in a curious reverent mood.

Our stay at camp is inclined to be a succession of small incidents. Nearby on the road to the Post Office is an old, nearly-demolished grist-mill and around its sagging framework grow abundant bushes, hanging down with juicy red raspberries. The taste is delightful and fresh, seeming so much more enjoyable when eaten from the bush. Not hygienic, of course, but we left the serious complex of hygiene in the porcelain bath at home.

The Post Office, barber shop and general store, and whatever other functions the building may serve, is a white business-dwelling house with a front porch so laden with the etcetera of a country store that were all the rest of the house to blow away it would not budge an inch! It is a country store dubbed as typical and having its share of homespun, cornbread philosophy and the interested gossip which makes all that is social of life in such a community. The Government has its pigeonholes in a corner across from the barber chair and the tall bottles of green liquids. Over and around, yes and under are: thread, onions, lamp globes, iodine, crab meat, gloves, dishes, brooms, spices, cinnamon bark, flour, veterinary medicine, fishhooks, canned peaches, rice and soap flakes. There seems to be one specimen of every known commodity of the last decade and somewhat previous. It is a real convenience, such a store. How the postmaster-barber-notary-proprietor ever finds the keys which go with the slim cans of Norwegian sardines is a wonder unequalled in any of the crossword puzzles ever published. The general man about the place doesn't hurry as he waits on us, but he always seems definitely on his way. He doesn't treat us deferentially but with a determined and sensible respect, quite superior to the saccharine attentions of the dapper clerk who sold us our shoes in town. He makes no pretexts and no guarantees; he sells, we buy!

. . .

This evening after a quiet boat ride along the indistinct glooms of the shoreline, we write and play cards or read as we do every other evening at camp. The absolute quiet is hourly punctuated by the boom of the town clock in the steeple of the white church in the village. Night isn't peaceful—rather it is *peace*.

. . .

Sometimes I hate these hills and feel almost aloof from them, but it is only because I know the deep hold they have on the very fiber of my being. The hills smile quietly on the many lives they hold in faithful trust. But usually I love the blue-green knobs of my hills and their quilted coverings of light green with the smocking of the deep evergreens. These hills hold pleasant treasures whether seen as a visitor or as a dweller along the lower sweep of their skirts. My hills hold a lake shaped like a giant *H*. Nearby at the bottom of a high slope is a brookside farm with bulky unpainted buildings.

Life is exceedingly serious here but yet it is companionable and healthful. There is something reassuring when one can look out daily onto the constancy of a hill—constant in the rain and in the snows. Sometimes—one is occasionally in the mood for it, one feels the sense of native allegiance to their motherhood as he climbs up the rocky breasts. I love the hump directly in front and across the lake from our camp. It is so reservedly and so stolidly friendly. It glowers on stormy days at the farm which has dared to crouch in the long grass at its foot—on sunshiny days it seems mildly amused in a satisfied way at those who in their comparatively few hours of their life wrench a living from its soil. Such a patient motherhood!

[130]

In the winter this same hill is beautiful but it demands stern purpose for those who wallow in its drifts. Although we may visit this in the softer beauty of the summertime we are not blind to the stiff work necessary for the cultivation of these mountainside fields and pastures. There is a joy of being and of growing but with it is the stern requirement that the hard phases of nature be met fairly. Nature doesn't know what graft means, and politics is not in her code of management. I often feel that the hills have come from the ancestry of the Western Highlands of Scotland, for they are of the same general shape, although the Scottish hills are more bare. The men are of the same determined and sturdy type.

One of the hills has a deep scar in its side where a few men are wresting talc from the hillside. Whereas we first felt it almost an insult to assail the hills in such a fashion, yet madame must have some charm lest man look more to the mountains than to her more perishable face.

Nightlong, quiet sleep and every breeze bringing the freshness from the brook beds and the elm groves. Morning, and unless it be especially gloomy or wet, it is announced in the different love and worship songs of the birds. Nothing ever seemed so eerie and dark as the windy blackness of a cloudy night. But sleep never seemed so much a delight. The air is a drug which brings simple rest to the day-tired body—without the complications of dreams. Instead I dream all day and rest at night. The dense oblivion of the night is a complete retreat to the original Faith which inspired even the hills.

. . .

Tonight it is cooler and clearer. A little distant lightning disturbs the sky occasionally but it is not bright enough to spoil the taffeta obscurity. When the boat is drifting and I lay my head face up to the sky, it seems as though I am being permitted to look at a rare sort of cinema. So many stars— some so large and some in a fine white spray. A falling star suddenly burning its way into oblivion startles me.

A distant jazz orchestra desecrates the solemnity of the night. There seems nothing so majestic as a cool clear autumn night. Soft white mists hover over the cooling water as pale lovers—so softly over the surface which has a sheen of unfathomable depths. In a way this evening is too big for me, there is too much of it, and I have not lived long enough in a conscious closeness to express it. That remains for some hill dweller who has turned his face many times to the autumnal stars. How mammoth is the conception of those tiny light flashes as other and larger worlds when I am so very much in the primer of this one.

We do not wish to leave this evening but yet we may see the crystal lights until the absolute seal of full slumber shall take us beyond them.

So cool, so crystal clear—so like the rustle of stiff taffeta—an autumn night.

. . .

Today we went onto the heights of the big mountain to the west to the "talc mine."

After we left the country store we climbed up into the clear warm sunshine—so hot that it burned our backs. Up into the dust of a country dirt road, where the jutting sizeable rocks gave the rider a jolt. We walked into the edges of the tall grass where we startled little brown birds who jerked out annoyed chirps at us until we were beyond the sound of their indignation.

The first farm welcomed us with its collie cow dog. It ran boldly out upon us—a veritable Roman, after the Gauls, but behind all that loud demand for our "Passports" was a bushy tail waving in a most friendly manner. I've known people like that who behind a gruff, reckoning front have real gentleness.

The hay recently cut sent up the fragrance of rich seeds and spices; crickets hummed away over to the blue hills in a long-drawn-out drone. One farmer in his south field drove his horses, hitched to the hayrack, like a skipper ordering a blunt Norwegian crew.

These farms seem funny if we look at them long. The first farm had a nice metal-roofed barn, unpainted but reasonably new. The house was a thing of patches. A red attenuated wooden structure which rambled on into a conglomeration of woodsheds and chicken houses. Lilac bushes grew clumped at the corner of the porch. Old hens pecked sedately among the long-legged adolescent chickens. The kitten found chance to display all the pouncing characteristics of the cat family on a very tiny victim, namely, a feather tossed by a chance breeze.

We really had to stop staring when the farm wife hung out her wash, so we walked out over the recently made stubble of a hayfield, then invaded the sanctum of two horses, via the barbed-wire fence route! Barbed wire causes more aching stitches for the farmer's wife's evenings than all the nails in the country. I usually don't bend low enough and the resulting r-r-r-r-ripping sound of the sliced and shredded cloth sends self-accusing qualms through me. The horses looked up, mildly curious, but certainly indifferent to my poor imitation of the drivers' "cluck." Then we went over a mossy stone wall, facing the ultramarine hills under the benediction-like shade of the broad beech leaves and into the outer woodland. We leaped rocks and brushed aside

[133]

branches and tossed away the long-reaching boughs of the hemlocks. Our careless boots cut swathes through the delicate sweet scented ferns which grow in a diffused matting everywhere. We plunged down-slope, now and then following a cowpath. We often came to little brooks and leaping them, we often landed ankle-deep in the black mud beyond, just missing the tufted clumps we had been leaping for. Nevertheless, we did find that dead sticks make a sort of summer snowshoe bearing us over the sloughs.

Windfall trees lay in scraggly heaps here and there. At the bottom of the slope was the inevitable marsh with the tall wire grass and the white beaks of the snake's-head herb. Blue flags tossed their thin strips into the wind. In the narrowest width of this spot we found a convenient bridge. This was a nearly decayed giant log. I owe it to these ruins of the forest to express gratitude for the many times they have borne me over murky places! Nature always gives support in all emergencies if we are moderately attentive. We soon knew that pasture land lay ahead, for we came upon a red cow, philosophically chewing some choice herbage and the tattered edges of this choice botanical specimen dangled in green shreds from her swaying mouth. Sure enough— beyond a copse of fir trees was the sugar place. This was evidently the back pasture of a farm and we climbed on until we came to the fields. Manipulating ourselves over a weak board fence we were on the edge of a field of green oats. While not particularly weary, yet the look over the country just traversed made us sit down in a half rest and half consideration of the distance behind and ahead.

How typical of Nature was its notice of us! We had just passed through those woods back there but no mark remained other than the trampled ferns and in three days those would right themselves. So much effort on our part and Nature had only been looking on very tolerantly!

We went on and if you accept that simple statement at its connotative value you have to pass over fences, stumps, and rocks, wet places and fallen trees. As we came through a farmyard we came to an old well. The wooden winch still hung punily over the dripping stone sides of this long tube into the earth. The house nearby was a gaping ghost building with a red tongue weakly stuck out—the leaning chimney, so long cold! In through its windows we could see tattered strips of paper falling from the old plaster. To think that once the neighbors said something like this: "Well did you see that new paper on Mrs. Farmer's parlor? It is a bit bright for such respectable people, but times aren't what they used to be!" And they must have said this in the early seventies.

Did you ever trail a country highway? Of course, we all have and know that there is something fascinating about the two sandy bands with grass between which undulate over the landscapes in twining and combining ribbons. A lot of real living has been done at the side of such roads—yes a bit of romance and then the final slow ride with real sorrow, to the white fenced acre at the crossroads. We took such a road to another abandoned farm.

There is something pitiful to me in an old house which has lost its windows and its doors, the top bricks from its chimney and its porch posts. It has been left to the enemy and the raspberries have invaded. The ridgepole sags. It is a decrepit old lady which has outlived its friends. But you know, the tiger and spotted lilies clamber all through the tall grass in a golden flourish of sympathy to the venerable bent-backed dame. Her husband the barn lies out yonder, already a heap of heavy bones—hand-hewn beams and pegged rafters. Inside the house the floors were a mess of old rags, traces of bird visitors, signs that a horse had been stabled in the old parlor, broken glass—a great litter. The

[135]

hedgehogs had eaten away the cellar stairs and etched the floorboards with the gnawing marks of their strong teeth; in their insatiable pursuit of a briney taste.

We now entered into a wood or logging trail. This climbed calmly into the forest and then twisted through the shade in the many convolutions of a big wet serpent, slipping between rocks and boulders. Once in a while we would slip into the mire but we penetrated farther into the shades and silences, now crossing a mountain brook in its tinkling hurry, then stepping warily over exposed roots—all of the fantasies that a thick first growth forest on a high mountain offers. Birds flew about at their business of living; once in a while snapping twigs betrayed unseen life close at hand. Piles of big logs awaited the winter's snow to be assimilated into the demands of civilization. This was just a respite in their giant aisles, granted by the seasons which do not tarry.

Finally we came out onto a good but corkscrew road around each corner of which we looked for the evidences of the "talc mine." Shortly around "the next corner" we came on the red stables, then to the foot of the red grinding-mill of our mine. Then came a disillusionment, for our late "talc mine" very innocently betrayed us by being an asbestos quarry. However the American flag snapping in the wind alleviated the shock, so rising to the occasion we surmounted the quarry. A rosy-cheeked foreman showed us the intricacies of his business, then selected us several samples of the unrefined ore full of the pale silky green fibers of the asbestos.

If you have ever turned suddenly face to face with a jewel case full of diamonds, you know how we felt when, turning, we found all New England spread out before us. As one friend said, "The blue Green Mountains galloped around the horizon." Yes, and so did the blue of the White Mountains and the Canadian Range. Between lay miles and

[136]

miles of woodland and farmland, over which spread miles and miles of tawny sunshine. These mountains swung as a gigantic deckled-edged scimitar against the wisped sky. We sighed and for once we didn't grope for adjectives. No use! We did not need to describe it. Its obviousness beggared any human tagging. Yet, here I am almost daring to label the crystallized ideas of a Great All in All.

We returned to the quarry and from the silvery interior of a Velvet Tobacco can we drank that cold pure liquid that is the breath of the hills. No drink like that from a mountain-side spring after the heated exertion of reaching it!

The leaving of such glory of revealed space is like the sad bon voyages of pierside—inevitable, but nonetheless pain-ful. We stepped again into the cool path of the forest. A chipmunk puckered up his face at us saucily; he jerked his tail as if to punctuate his disdain. Across the path another chipmunk emerged from the mould under a log pile to perch on the end of a long log and give us the "once-over." He departed! The first one of the family turned around, face to us as we passed him, as much as to say, "Well, well, run along now! I can't waste any more of my time watching you tall heavy-walking trees!"—hoping that I am translating the latest in the Chipmunk circle. It is all a part of the unwritten but nonetheless existent code of the forest. I once had an aunt—a dear old grand-aunt who was just such a perky wee creature.

When we passed again the old house among its lilies we followed a semi-washed-out road into the woods. So little was it used that low branches met overhead in a green net. We knew that someone had recently passed that way, for fresh unwilted leaves were scattered along the middle of the path. In the dark swamps at the side grew the tall ferns, spreading out their perfect fronds into a tropic semblance. In some places we almost seemed to be looking back into the

[137]

damp Carboniferous period. The road ran on and on, up and down over bumps, into gullies and beside moss-draped boulders. At a length measured not in miles or time, but in the growing pain of our legs, we came to another asbestos mine on a farther hillside but showing no evidence of recent operation, and at a much lower level than our "talc mine."

We snubbed it and followed one country road into another. We passed seven or eight abandoned farms sitting helplessly in fields of over-ripe hay. So hollow-cheeked— these grey old houses, paneless and paintless. One or two seedy apple trees remain faithful but degenerate. It seems a sad condition that a nation should have so many of its back farms slipping back into the wild stage. Yet what can hold people to the backwoods when the way out is so easy? We must need more seriousness of purpose.

Our fifteen miles added to our hunger and made the soft lengths of bed most inviting—and then there was the silent starlight where we could think it all over. Today I had learned more of my wonderful country and had walked next to it unafraid.

. . .

Several miles from our camp, far away across the cloud-shadowed hillsides there is a deserted village. The people took all their possessions and left, and now for years at the mouth of an unused asbestos mine, the wooden buildings of the mine town have stood slipping deeper and deeper into the raspberries and thrifty grass. Big white clouds spread soft shadows as they sailed along, and the intensity that such solitude has made the place seem a spectre. Well, we can see that it is not close to the realm of little boys, for the panes of glass are intact. Most of the houses are open and birds build their nests on the floors. Hedgehogs and all small animals make their regular excursions within.

Someone or some people a long time ago tried to make a go of a big venture but the vein of asbestos ran out, and the workers left to the enclosing solitudes their homes where children once played and dogs barked. All falls into despair then disrepair. A few apple trees are the only touches left of the dead community. We sped away after picking a few raspberries. Tonight under the cool stars we know of the few bulky man-made shadows out there in the dew—few others know of it. We shall probably never visit it again but there it is—the village that is dead. Again the silent hills tolerate but slowly erase. The stars will look down still when every ridgepole has sagged to the ground and then the trees will close over the town that used to be.

· · ·

We like trailing from car or on foot into the beautiful thrills of the unexpected.

We went to Canada—to the touch which is so significantly British which shows both in people and their dwellings. And officialdom is in its glory at the borders of our two countries. It isn't such a gold braid officialdom, but rather a blunt-jawed efficiency. I do not expect the fish in the creek between the two giant countries have any international complications although they may hold anti-fishhook and line conferences to uphold the trend of the times.

Many of my fellow countrymen flock to the other side and find many things different. I never found the air more rarified though possibly a little more *spirited*. Bees hum around a hive as tourists do around the beer dispensary in Rock Island.

. . .

We are sitting here in the quiet orchestration of the rain. It makes a whole octave on the various leaves and on the roof of our porch. I write letters to friends and wish each one were here. I could not wish them all here together for good friends are complements of our insufficient self and as such can each be enjoyed best separately.

The rain has washed away the haze and the hills are ranked in true perspective for my review. They leap above each other until the pale blue mounds of the farther hills nose into the grey sky. On rainy days Nature cleans up. How appropriate that it should rain on a Saturday!

. . .

Today I found the story back of our "deserted village." A kindly old gentleman with one arm missing told me as we sat together on his porch, in the back seat and frame of an ancient Ford automobile.

Many years ago a wise old judge deserted the bar to work six hundred acres of mountain land, which he had come into the possession of. He had "lumbered it off" for some four or five years when asbestos was discovered. A mine grafter found out about the discovered seam and paid the judge a fine sum for a half interest. The judge was a crafty man and used to go into the neighboring state with his trunk about the time of the town "listing" of property and remain there until after the taxation was due, thus saving on taxes. Being

[140]

constantly at swords' points with the man who held half interest, the judge sold out his remaining half and divorcing his wife, who had been faithful to him during his lumbering years, he was last seen with a young girl of a wife in a neighboring state. Exit the judge!

The new mine owner went into his venture in an excited inflation—fully but not wisely. He erected many buildings out there on that lonesome mountain, with many improvements, putting in much machinery which was inferior. Among many things which he failed in, he was a wretched manager. He had a good vein there, and today one that is said to be superior to the mine which is being operated on the other face of the mountain, but he was not able to get it out fast enough to make ends meet. He allowed his accounts at stores to grow and grow, until he ruined the poor grocer who had trusted him, by an account due of fourteen hundred dollars. He left many other debts and went to a distant city where he has wisely remained since. His workmen still are unpaid their later wages. The sister of this man backed the proposition and died in financial distress. There the village and the mine stand, accumulating taxes, and the buildings sinking into the disrepair of desertion. Homes, hearts, money, lives—all sacrificed on the hearth of industry and we saw only a crumbling pitiful group of isolated houses. We feel it now to have a more solid spectre than ever!

. . .

The storekeeper here near camp is a fiddler. For many years, until his health gave out, he rode over the hills to play for the kitchen junkets and the barn dances. He held a dancing school. He told me that once he used to go over the

East Hill, and all were great fertile farms. Today only one of nine is still occupied and the banks holding the foreclosure mortgages on the others are weakened by them.

The storekeeper knows all the lore of the countryside. This particular bit is connected with the mountain of our disillusioning "talc mine." This mountain of the Sun (for its name is that of the God of the Dawn) was once visited by the Indians who went yearly from lake to lake on a trail of their own, years before the railroad and while the storekeeper was very young. On their annual trek northward they brought lead which they bartered for products. When asked where it came from, they would make a gesture to the mountain and say nothing more. Men have searched much over the Mountain of the Sun but never have they seen lead. The last of the Red-Skins has long been dead, and with him went the secret of the lead mine on the Mountain of the Sun.

The storekeeper says there must be riches deeper than the asbestos. Maybe so! At least there is a richness in these legends of the Mountain of the Sun.

. . .

The sky is in the midst of a turmoil. The fierce fires of Heaven are seaming, creasing, splitting, fretting and smocking the dark garments of the Firmament. At intervals the trees and leaves are stamped in a coarse fillet against the hem of Heaven. There is the heavy droning in the distance of a thousand thundering bees. Unseen chariots are assailing the Universe of rough cobblestones. The entire sky is being reflected by the surprised lake, as it whirls in a vivid Apache dance. A band of ancient Indians are returning to their hunting grounds with the heavy beating of Tom-Toms.

[142]

The lake is at odd moments endowed with all the glory of a golden sunset, then plunged into a black that seems twice as deep because of the recent gold. We are given quick intimate glimpses of the hills in their night composure. Nature is throwing off a mood with a tortuous convulsion.

Now the drums roll more distant and the flashing searchlights weaken as they dissect the piled-up clouds. The sky has become a black marble tabletop off which the heavy iron saucepans are being swept by the hurrying housemaid—the wind. The clouds are now tearing apart and the moon peers through.

Nature sinks to a very deep rest after her grandiose gesture!

. . .

I went down to the village last night to get the late mail. It was very dark; the brook alongside the road rushed about its affairs with the big stones in its bed, quite undetected. The skeleton of the old mill stood clothed with a sense of mystery in its fringe of dark fingered trees.

The store was a live spark in the black pit of a huge cooling furnace. One good neighbor sat softly on a pile of overalls, while another assumed temporary regency in the one barber chair. The air was blue with smoke and comments. A hill farmer, on a back-road farm, was giving his *set* opinions of the road commissioner and they were largely along the line of destructive criticism.

The postmaster-storekeeper-barber was behind his pigeonholes sorting the mail. The bulk of the two bags was a large number of mammoth catalogues from a distant mail-order house.

One man came out from a private consultation with the

postmaster, bearing his catalogue which the rest scanned over his shoulder. He turned to the fine fences pictured between fields which in smoothness and extent could not be found within two hundred miles. He eyed them critically, then gave his judgement: "I cal'late that I'd better fence the North Field since that brown yearlin' has torn down the board fence. She's the derndest critter for gettin' into the oats, I ever see!"

"How's you oats comin' anyway, John? Mine was all beat down by the rain last Sunday and some of 'em don't look like they was goin' to straighten up."

"Mail's ready. Here's a letter for Mary, John."

I took my letter and accompanied the sun-browned boy of a hill farmer part of the way. He didn't say much but swung along with the easy grace of one used to long hill stretches. He was utterly unconscious that he had the features of a Greek Apollo. We parted with a cursory "Good night!" I wonder if his thoughts went beyond the horizon of the hills, for he made me wander again on a mountain road descending from a high pass, far beyond these hills and much water.

. . .

One early learns at camp the exceptional beauty of the early morning, a beauty consistent with the reflections of a crystal. Yet we have also learned the art of lying half-awake in bed and enjoying the morning. The sleeping porch opens onto the fresh bosom of a woodland. It touches the house with the soft boughs of the spruces. That reverie which is popularly reserved for the twilight we get as the natural course of our first view into the pure perspective of the morning. Every moment seems a cornucopia of possibility!

This morning I closed my eyes after the first view of the day and reviewed in sweet delicious half slumber, the golden points of a recent tour through woodlands akin to these but many compass degrees away. I felt again the breezes of mountains far higher, not because of dissatisfaction here but because my surroundings here interpret the deeper values of the other environments. At the end of each trail there should be a period of interpretation and absorbtion which will make for the permanent retainment of the markers along the trail. I here am having my happy siesta and enjoying the after-glow of the sunny days along the big trail.

. . .

There is a man in the village who has the reputation of being a sort of a prophet. He lost his left arm in a sawmill years ago and has now slipped easily into old age. He is one who really "lives in a house by the side of the road" and I believe he is "a help to man." Between whiffs of pipe smoke from a very strong pipe, he ejects his comments and opinions. Then he listens very well; in fact, listening is an art with him. Every remark which he chooses to make we always know is the product of years of careful listening. Every small town has its sage but we think ours is the best. We have only to hint at tomorrow's weather and he will lay it out before us, and be it said to his credit—it is rarely far off the actual. His mind is a veritable list of dates. He knows when everyone in town was born, who their parents were, how much they are worth and where the absent ones live. He has been a great help to me for he has interpreted the entire horizon of hills into the vernacular of local lore. He knows the legends and the history which clothes meaningless places into gold mines. Life really has assumed more meaning since this kindly one-armed prophet has given his opinions of it.

. . .

The weather is very cloudy today, threatening rain but never quite coming to its production. Nevertheless the Soldier[1] and I made an inspiring hike over a rugged mountain. Tonight I know my hills better for having weathered their stouter slopes and I know the lake better for having seen it with the haughty eyes of the hills, as they look down upon it. It is a haughter of position rather than a lack of sympathy.

The Soldier has a good West Point stride. Together we went through the woods on a logging trail, determined that Mt. Norris should fall before our advance. At some distance along this lumber-trail we came to a cleared place, a fern-carpeted clearing, in the midst of which we found a set of buildings in the last attempt to keep upright. The hedgehogs have chewed a good portion of the stairs away. Near the sagging doorstep one hedgehog had met with an untimely death and lay flattened out in a mesh of black and white quills. On the corner rock of the barn foundation a sizeable snake lay out full length catching the benefit of the sun, which burst the clouds with its rays every so often. As we approached the checkered reptile slid out of sight. Men and snakes keep up the Biblical convention of enmity!

A few tiger lilies blossomed cheerily, as though the hands of yesterday might touch and pick them.

We struck into the woods. Forests have characteristics which are quite human. At their outset they are wide,

[1]Lt. Frank Ruggles, then a student at West Point. (Ed. note.)

[146]

spaciously shaded with soft beds of fern; so cool and so inviting. The deeper one goes within the more intriguing they are, and the more difficult; unsuspected characteristics are encountered. As we mounted higher we had to work harder. We fell and crawled over the branches left by last year's lumbermen. I could not help but compare this seeming waste after clean woodlands of the Black Forest and the Bernese Alps. Sometimes we reached for sticks to have them topple over on us in rotten weakness.

It is now the season when birches put on their newest white. Their last year's robes hang in tatters along the trunk for the sport of the prying wind. Christmas ferns make dark green motifs on an oriental carpet of greens, grays and browns.

I stepped on a rock covered with a rich moss, when all in a moment I found myself sitting on both legs in the underbrush. Apparent at once that wet stones do not hold their moss fast. After many more moments of perspiring exertion we climbed out on the top—a great bare ledge. The lake lay far, far below like a giant letter H. The surrounding hills seemed more squat when we looked on them from above. We turned north but alas, there ahead was the top, many hundred feet up. How vain were our visions of having reached it.

We climbed on, stepping gingerly along ledge faces, catching live boughs for support, then pushing our way through the rigid low branches of the rough spruce. These dead lower branches make natural barriers which tear and scratch as we inch our way through them. We reached another top only to be disillusioned as before.

At last after following a newly trodden path through the ferns we came out on another top—the real top, this time. There were too many spruces to permit of a good view. We found the rock where the Soldier and his companions had carved their names in 1925, with the case of an exploded shotgun shell. I added my initials and left it to the witnessing of two hawks that were wheeling and screaming overhead. I am sure it will be many moons before I shall revisit this lofty autograph collection.

We descended by a more precipitous route. The spruces just below the summit have been assailed by a tremendous storm in years past, and now they lean toward the summit rocks. One tall spruce stood with a fresh burned stripe down from its top to the ground. Thin splinters and bits of bark lay on the ground, around this lightning conductor.

Downward we fell, scrambled, jumped and scurried over the ledges and piles of rock, under which were many small caves suitable for homes of the small game. Hedgehogs live in those caves and the gnawing of their strong teeth has etched the trunk of many a tree in the vicinity. These bristling pincushions are voracious. We came suddenly to the abrupt edge of a ledge and saw many feet below the rocky undergrowth. We went cautiously along the edge until we could let ourselves down the side with the aid of branches. We dropped ten feet to the level and looked back up at the precipice. Along its weather-carved face were nitches where the dark evergreen trees found a precarious foothold.

The Soldier and I stumbled on until another old logging road led us to pastureland. We followed a cowpath onto the highway; two scratched, tired trampers. Across the highway is a very cool spring gushing out of the rocks in a small cold stream. We drank deep and swung down the road. Tourists came rolling by, seeing the country in the luxury of their cushions. Truly they saw the hill, but we knew it. We had worked for a closer acquaintance with it and were rewarded. Those who rush through in such a way are content with outward appearances alone.

Tired? Perhaps, but with the full satisfaction which comes

of climbing over the big hills. The Soldier is a good hiker. My definition of a good hiker is a man or woman who can walk long miles over rough ground and in rough costume, who can assail the hills and then absorb a view without an explosion into adjectives, then retreat gracefully.

. . .

Tonight I feel all the significance of the Moonlight Sonata. I sit all alone on the bow of my beached boat and look out over the great piece of glossy black satin. The moon is only an hour high over the dark points of the steepled spruces. There is a soft thin mist that rises from the cooling lake. Out of the opaque shadows there come two silent flitting night birds, and disappear as silently. As the water laps the smooth stones of the shore the movement makes six small reflected moons do a symphonic dance. My shadow runs long and slender back of me over the stones. Across the lake, in the feathery foliage of the white birches are the few lights of the half-hidden cottages.

The night is serene and makes me think of things not exactly tangible. I gaze in wonder, as if never aware that lakes wear the moonlight thus and as though I never had seen the full lunar blossom over quiet waters. It is not so, but each fullness of the moon seems as though a new miracle and makes me wonder at life, at the hills, and think of those scenes and figures which are very far distant. It is a time for remembering; remembering friends and places. It is also a period when the question of the future seems so vague to me. Sometimes I think it would be good if we might periodically gain our full realization of an aim then take another aim; to a certain extent we do this and then again, it would be an unprogressive way. The moon is a candle for the dreamer, a torch for the poet, a symbol for the lover; even a deity for the superstitious. The very practical man rarely profits directly from the moonlight, but has it to work with in the dreams transmitted from the dreamer.

. . .

Away out on the back roads there are many farms where life is drudgery and the gains of the farming are barely sufficient to make the ends meet. The houses are unpainted, the lawns unmowed. Old piles of wood and pieces of rusty machinery are in the front dooryard. Milk cans and an impoverished washing grace the leaning porch. The windows boast no lace curtains, the roof is patched with tin. This is life in its hardest. Yet women live in those houses and bear children and die. Women love beauty; it is the nature of their souls. A tired backwoods farmwife can only show her touch of the eternal feminine with the greatest effort. She has no gowns to display, her hats are even archaic. Yet I saw today in these backwoods homes windows full of red geraniums, and tall burning crimson hollyhocks by the withered weathered clapboards. These are holy flowers. They come from the impoverished souls of people off the beaten highway. The woman might be very embarrassed if confronted by her display consciously, yet rough and hard-driven mother though she be, her geraniums have burned into the sense of what is fine and holy. They are sterling expressions of a silent long-suffering, even unrecognized craving for the infinity of beauty.

. . .

[150]

Once back against the bank of the brook that hurries under a bridge and through the village from the mill, there stood a tin-type shop. That was very many moons ago. No one lives in the width of these valleys who can remember the place, but mouth-to-mouth legend-telling of long winter evenings have kept the story for us. Here in this small house lived an old man and his dog. He had a wife but didn't get along with her particularly well and found better company in his uncomplaining dog. The old man used to make and mend shoes, then besides his cobbling he was a great hunter and fisherman.

Today as in those days there are many miles of wild woodland called the South Woods. These woods are filled with the story of a great bog where animals are sucked down alive. Many great unaccountable things have their supposed origin in the South Woods. This old man used periodically to go to visit his wife in a small village to the southeast. He would take his dog and disappear for days at a time, always going in the direction of the South Woods. After a while he would return to his tin-type house and his cobbling.

One time the old man went away and didn't come back for a long time. Then one night on a hill above the brook which raced by the tin-type shop, a dog stood and howled. It was the old cobbler's dog! It howled several nights there and then disappeared. A posse of three hundred men was gathered and they beat the South Woods by night and day for several days to no avail. Neither dog nor master was ever found. But far in these rarely-visited forest stretches they came on the great swamp. They decided that the old man had come on this in the night and fell victim to the sucking mire. A few still aver that he was murdered, yet who would wish to murder a poor old cobbler who took to the woods with his dog? And where did the dog disappear to?

[151]

There today in tranquil greenness are the South Woods but there is around the village a deep awe of the shades of this great forest.

. . .

We have at last found a talc mine. It was two score miles from the disillusioning asbestos mine. We found it in a valley which a few years ago was swept by a very destructive flood. All the farmhouses along the valley are tilted at dizzy angles. Many are uninhabitable and sit sideways on their weak foundations. Wreckage of barns still strews the valley meadows. In the towns paint is peeling off the houses up to the second story, which was the water level.

We went into a powdery white building and climbed up several flights of slippery stairs. Everything that this powdered talc settles on becomes very slippery. We went up past the great grinders which crumble the rock to a very fine powder. At the top of the many stairs we entered the dumping room which is level with the mine. Here were several cars loaded with the mineral waiting for dumping into the big hoppers. Two young miners turned these cars, the men wearing little star-like lamps on their caps.

We went into the mine. Very cool air met us and it seemed to get colder as we walked into the shaft which is horizontal. On and on we went, along the slippery track, into the heart of the mountain. The damp talc underfoot was very tricky. The walls glistened pale greenish-white in the electric light glare. We saw the pieces being picked off with the sharp steel tools and the drills working with the savage sound of machine guns.

We came back out and went to the cutting room where the talc is cut by saws into little square shapes and also into

[152]

pencils for marking fine marbles. This very fine grade talc is a pale luminous green and feels like soap. Light can be seen through pieces of it a quarter of an inch thick.

Once more in the open we scuffed our feet in the grass to clean off the talc and shook off the fine white powder. We have thus seen Dame Nature's boudoir!

. . .

Today we left Eden for a few hours and took to the higher levels. We went along the valley to the foot of Jay Peak. This peak is only some 3860 feet high but after the ascent and descent it is several thousand feet higher in its toll of sore muscles. There is a fine trail up this mountain. It is the Long Trail which leads over the higher peaks of this New England state. Long—indeed it is, and after toiling over wet stones and muddy spots we prepared for the view from the top but alas, the top loomed up seemingly thousands of feet ahead.

A disturbed squirrel was the only one who noticed us. No birds appeared. We walked on up and up, easily following the carefully made trail; and may the trail-maker receive herewith our thanks for his foresight. As we neared the top the trees grew leaning toward the mountainside. Stunted but old spruces crept in line with the rocks. The top is largely snowy white quartz with small sedge plants growing in the nitches. Here and there were tufts of withered grass. A cool wind swept briskly over the summit.

The view! Two countries and their districts for a hundred miles around lay out clear and pleasant before us. To the west under the notched peaks of the Adirondacks lay a long lake. To the east were other lakes and a distant ridge or comb of blue mountains. Another lake pierced the great Dominion to the north. The faint smokes from the busy towns of two friendly countries came from the lowlands. Rivers snaked along, sometimes behind lesser hills. Geography lay before us and the full-breasted richness of our country.

We descended and met others toiling up as we had done. They greeted us and inquired as to the distance to the top. We knew; but lest they be discouraged we said, "Not far." At the bottom of the trail runs a very clear icy brook. It looks like clear crystal laid over pebbled amber. Deep masses of ferns sweep both sides of this mountain stream. We had come to the end of the trail but we had been up in the rafters of our country and had looked over the massive framework of the hills. We came back happy in the knowledge that all was well in Creation, even with us, the Created.

. . .

We have just had an old folks' dance in the town hall. This town hall is the large rectangular room over the school-rooms, where the ordeal of town meeting is celebrated. The orchestra was a double attraction, the first being the piano, the second being the fiddle. This latter instrument was similar in every way to a violin as long as it was silent, but once the bow fell on the strings it wheezed and coughed out moans and tired notes and weary wails. Together time was created for the dancing. All the village was there; the little French girl at the Inn, the farmer's boy with the freckles, the storekeeper's daughter. They seemed very embarrassed in their good clothes and somewhat ill-at-ease. The dances were square dances. Perhaps. But every way I attacked them I got circled into a mess that I never righted until the dance stopped. The calling of the moves confused me. I reached for the wrong hand of the wrong person. I consistently did the wrong thing and at the wrong time. My head swam but my feet kept time to the noise though never for long in the right direction. There was one consolation: some of the village youths didn't do much better and we all had a laugh at each other. Coffee and cake required no special technique and along about eleven-thirty we went home.

If these highly intricate movements constitute square dancing then I am all for round dancing. They belong in the hills, these dances, but I have not been here long enough yet to have become master of all the ritual! My mother did these, my grandmother did these, but will my grandson ever see them?

. . .

Up on a hill above the lake two Sisters from a city far to the west have bought an abandoned farm and are now trying to evolve a home from it. The Sisters have never married and their life has been largely that of the schoolroom.

They are great walkers, these Sisters. They have walked to the next village and back, some twenty miles in all, though both have grey hairs beyond count. They love the outdoors and their type of outdoor work is the juice of the rural conversation. Local comment has the ladies in all stages of insanity: "What did they want that old place for?" "They must be funny, wanting to fix up that old farm!" "City folks are always doin' the golramdest things a body ever thought of." "Think of two women doin' sech a fool thing! You'd think they'd want comfort instead of workin' all the time around that old place, but they don't seem to do nothin' sensible. The idea walkin' up to the top of them rocks jest to see the sun set. My sakes, they can't be very busy!" These and other comments are the characteristic reactions of the village people. They are rather suspicious of us who have the leisure of a month, anyway. Their idea of a vacation is a day's trip on an excursion, or more likely a day's trip to some distant relative "a visitin'."

Yesterday I went up to the Sisters' home and saw the sunset. The mountains stood in a deep Prussian blue line against a burnished orange sky. They were so clear that they seemed cut out and pasted on the firmament. When I reached this hill-top farm one of the Sisters, the younger, was busy on her stone wall. Across the entire front lawn at the road edge she has built a strong stone wall. This disturbs the hill people. They think it may make the snow drift into the road, so comment is caustic on this fine wall. Stones, and there are many around, have been especially chosen for size, shape and lichen growths, to go into this wall. Planning and strenuous effort have made it the success that it is. All along it grow peonies and golden glow. These latter have their gold blossoms now at the top of the tall stalks. Along here is to be a "friendship garden." Each of their friends will be asked to contribute a plant or shrub—then there will grow the rows of friends, ever present, subject to the winds and weather.

The Sisters have pulled the old wallpaper off and tinted the walls in their house. Not being in affluence they cannot get antique period furniture for the house but instead they are having everything rough, crude and comfortable. An old cheese-press is in the process of evolution into a table. The old churn has developed into a suitable sewing table. And the old wooden washing machine has been coaxed into the distant semblance of a dressing table. True that the plans of the Sisters call for extensive things to be done and for a long time, but what is life without its visions and what dream is nobler than the metamorphosis of a house into a home?

They take time off to get close to the hills, they study the people in a sympathetic way and if they stick to it, the village people will be for them. Country people are not rushed into new situations but accept them when the permanence is assured. We need more such women and men with foresight and a desire for a home to bring these sleeping old farms back to the smile of life.

. . .

I go this afternoon to see the pasture. This is a veritable chimera of delectable objects. The raspberry bushes are nearly barren but still hold one or two of their heavy red tokens for me. The blackberries on their taller bushes are just changing a rich red for a glossy black. They are there for me but I must pay toll in the breaking through the obstinate thorns of these sturdier bushes. The red berries of the blackberry are very hard and sour but those already black are luscious and leave drippings of rich violet on my hand.

Everywhere there is a softness from the ferns. They stand like slender soldiers doing graceful guard duty. Each symphonic creation stands there in dainty erectness. They are soft and crumple easily with a pungent odor.

From the rocks the view is hazy. A pale blue diffusion is on the distant hills and the high ones nearer are light ul-tramarine, as if disintegrating into the warm afternoon air. Crickets drone and a tall group of purple thoroughwort bears in its plumes a host of bumblebees humming about their sweet business. The white or pearly everlastings stand as spectres among the bright flash of the goldenrod; yet that bright gold will be a rotting brown while these white papery blossoms are still standing in the early snows. The "soon-dying among the ever-living." But the goldenrods are the show of the pasture. They ramble along the stone wall, they

[157]

possess the edges of the marsh. They rise straight from the tall grass at the side of the beaten cow-path. They descend the hill in bobbing gilt ranks. Here and there are lone purple sentinels bristling with arms. These great thistles bear proudly the traditions of their family. They bear their royal color with distinction and with protection; they command a dignified approach.

Back of me three tall spruces have made a deep shade with their lower boughs. They sweep in a deadness the entire ground and nothing green grows under this shade. All is needles and soft aromatic silence. It is a perfect shelter and a real place of rest. A few cows browse half-heartedly in the lower meadows among the remnants of the buttercups.

This is peace of late summer. A long droning afternoon without purpose or direction. Everything before one but no necessity of doing any more than absorb easily the whole atmosphere of teeming abundance.

. . .

There are herearound many small sounds which I hear and enjoy as a child. They are insignificant but vivid tones of nature. One is the dead click of two stones rapped together under water. Another is the whispering of the breeze through the soft ferns when one lies among them. The other is the natural song of melancholy—the purring of the wind through the pine trees. Then the water as it laps the drip-ping stones. Distant voices that cry beyond the horizon; music of the deep woods and great distances. Woodpeckers that make staccato tom-toms on the big trees. Brooks drip in melody through the weeds. Life here on the lake has a thousand almost-whispers which are waiting for detection. They are the fine accompaniments of the great pastoral.

. . .

I went walking through the woodland this morning with the Spanish poet who has just come. He found many delightful thoughts in the woods. As we crossed the road to the shore he noticed all the little rolled-up bits of dust and said, "Each is a little world, with its own shadow." Then when we [were] going through the thickets of dogwood he said that these were the protestations of the woodland that its virginity be unviolated by we trespassers. One decaying stump was for him the ruin of a citadel of Babylon, another became a castle. It was soft nearly in powder and the poet, great child that he and all poets are, knelt and shaped of the white punk material a castle. He covered it with moss and there it stood—first a mere rotten birch stump, now a historic castle of the plains of La Mancha in faraway Spain. He watched me push over a few rotted trees and he said I was a Cyclops intent on destroying the weak and unfit. In other words what had always been a lovely woodland to me had become for him something symbolic.

It is a glorious day and the woods are in the last reverie of summer. There are many branches of brilliant scarlet and of magenta which show us that the first frosts have left their caresses. Yet in the deep woodland it is as ever, half gloom and the whispering carpet of last year's leaves.

We came out into a forest clearing and found by cellar holes that in the last century there had been a road here and many farms. Now it is an abandoned memory. A few old

[159]

apple trees stenciled by the sharp bills of the woodpeckers still do a lonesome vigil. Wild roses now have their red berries which the maids about make into chains of gigantic red beads for their dolls. Goldenrods rose in plumy extravagance on every side. A few tall mullen plants bore up their yellow tipped stock from their velvet leaves. Still lingered a few of the feathery thoroughwort. Giant blue asters stretched tall and brilliant in the fall sunlight.

How rare was all this to the poet from Spain! He said that when we were talking so joyfully in English he would converse with the dog, who was very *simpático*. But he entered into all the sport. Never is he without a joke and he said after looking all around the adorned room that it was so significantly the farewell to the summer that his feet were cold!

We walked in the field back of the house and picked blackberries and blueberries. We picked the small hard fruit of the neglected orchard to make into spicy applesauce. The poet meanwhile was making a masterpiece, not in poetry but in floral design. From a simple base of pearly everlastings he added golden sprays of goldenrod and the tall spike of a mullen, a few deep red leaves from a raspberry bush, a bunch of red elderberry and back of this a spray of pine branches, among which he put long stalks of ripe timothy grass. It was a beautiful thing to look at and appeared as a mirror of the Season. The final touch was a group of three small branches with little apples. The poet bore it as his offering to the feast.

And feast it was. Steaming platters of creamed chicken with many cups of jasmine tea went quickly the way of the homemade cookies and the rare sandwiches. Then the poet sang us the native songs of Andalusia and we retaliated with the plantation songs and the old songs of our country. He

[160]

appreciates our rich background, which so many do not believe that we have.

The afternoon sky became a heavy-blanketed mat from which a month later we would expect snow. This feast was filled with a certain pathos. It was a farewell to each other, for the coming week would find us all in different places and with our minds full of other affairs. Not long until this lone house on the hill will receive the deep vigils of the snows and the blue hills will pass into a glory of white, and we will be far away—remembering.

We were sitting quietly when the poet made a sort of delighted gulp and started for a small maple standing head high in the rank grass. It was a tongue of absolute crimson. Beside it was another miracle. This was a long cobweb of some six feet between the maple and an old dock plant. The spider chose the dock plant for his landscaping but had run his foundation across to the fiery maple. We lifted this up, this silken-threaded barrier and went under. Yes, we could have easily broken it, but one doesn't break things ruthlessly on so perfect a morning. Man has left the field to the small creatures and so we left it. It was a gigantic oriental carpet intoned with the deep browns and siennas of the autumn.

Autumn, the time when nature takes inventory and flames forth her abundance. The hours when she poises taut, then plunges into the preparation for the quiet solitudes of winter. Autumn, when we must leave the garden of Eden and dream on the things we have drunk so deeply of.

. . .

Sally is another local saint. Saints most always come from the lowly people, those who have been intensely human.

Joan of Arc was such and so is Sally. I hereby canonize her. There are those still living who remember Sally well. She was an old woman when they knew her, a bent old woman who limped, and had grey hair, deep-set eyes and the very perfection of a smile. She lived in the house where the two Sisters from the far West now live.

How was she a Saint? To begin with her life was only that of the farm wife back on the hill roads, barren enough of outward sentiment. But Sally loved children—and children are always a way to saintly happiness and sainthood. She used to meet the children as they went by her house on the long mile or two miles that they had to go to school and she never met them single-handed. In the fall and the late spring Sally brought out cups of cool water drawn from the water barrel where the water always ran and still is running. The Sisters have kept it so for they reverence Sally. In the winter she used to have them come in and warm themselves, these children of the back hills. Her cookies and doughnuts became famous.

How strange it must have seemed when Sally died and the children who had grown up under her kindly ministrations passed the house with its empty panes. She is the cherished memory of many a household now far remote and ah, what a stronger marker is this example than the greatest shaft of lordly granite. Sally—daughter of the harsh and homely hills but one who drank from them their protective meaning and let it radiate, honor to you, Saint Sally of Eden!

. . .

The poet of Spain has been comparing things today, especially as to his environment of Andalusia and our hill-embraced lake. Our hills are lower and greener. They are not the mystic snow-capped elegance, that of the Sierra back of Granada, but they give another sentiment, a feeling of infinite comfort. His vega or plain of olive trees has here given way to the rolling hay fields and the knolls dotted with appletrees and boulders. The oranges, lemons and limes are here apples and currants. He is delighted, the dreamer of all that is ancient Granada, to find here the *zarzamora* of Andalusia, that is, the blackberry. Then we have the raspberries and blueberries which he is less acquainted with. He sees a bush, a familiar tree and the momentary homesickness which we are all prey to takes him and he looks with saddened eyes far far beyond the thicket. Who of us, who have been in his suave and sunny land have not at odd minutes found a strain of music, a voice or the notes of a bird, enough to set our hearts beating a little faster? Yet one would not know the correct valuation of home unless he could cross to these lands and have this occasional nostalgia. But he likes our hills and writes of them, does this poet of Spain.

. . .

This country is alive to the limit with legends. Our latest discovery is the Garden of Eden. Up on the East Hill which borders on the mystic South Woods, on a hill infamous for its roadway condition there is a patch of wonderful garden. Just now this piece of isolated beauty is far beyond its best, for the village folks who have seen it say that late May and early June find it thus. This is off the main road and comparatively isolated, in fact difficult to get at. The average hill dweller in passing with a visitor, simply points out

[163]

toward the wilderness and says that the Garden of Eden is there. He may have been there once when deer-hunting or he may only have heard of it from John who lives down in the old red house, or Mary, she that used to live in the house over that cellar hole upon the knoll, she that had ten children and died bearing the eleventh; she may have been there once when berrying, to feed her many hungry mouths.

The village muse told us that once Indians had maintained a settlement here and these were their records, these semi-cultivated flowers which, using the native richness of the fertile soil have become such hardy perennial blossomers. However we found in that legend-hallowed acre that there were traces of a very old set of buildings there. Probably in the late eighteenth century the seeds were strewn which still make for the spring time glory which many tell of and very few have seen. It is so much easier to accept a thing as so, than to search it out for ourselves. I know, for I too have taken geometry!

. . .

Ceres and Bacchus celebrated with us the advent of the Autumn. We found the Gods of the harvest at the house of the two Sisters. The first kisses of the frost have sufficiently turned the leaves that the simple dining room of this erstwhile abandoned house was a great flame of delicate red and rich brown. Deep brown fronds of the frost-caressed ferns made lacy shadows on the tinted walls.

. . .

[164]

The poet from Spain calls so many things *simpático,* that I sometimes have desired to know the full value of this rich word. Tonight I found it out.

We were coming back from the post office, with no light. The road was dark and the river ran menacingly. Not one star gave its blue point of light above the hills and everything was a great void in which we wandered as lost souls. We heard not long after crossing the river the crunch of fellow footsteps and from the dark spoke a kindly "hello." We spoke of the weather and then he recognized us, this as yet unknown walker, since we were speaking Castilian. He asked questions about the country of Spain. He expressed the quaint idea that the chief reason for raising children in Spain was to see who could raise the most beautiful children.

An automobile rounding the corner of the trees showed our kindly friend. He was the large and bewhiskered watch repairer of the village. His smile was contagious. After more words we went our ways into the deepness of the night.

The Spanish friend said, "¡Qué simpático!"—and I then understood.

. . .

Today we are to leave Eden. The almanacs say that the first day of Autumn is a good month off but my hills didn't consult the almanac. They have already raised their brightest plumage in many spots. Of course the forest isn't the silent flame that it will be a month hence but it has now the mottled look of a grandmother's crazy-patchwork quilt.

We do not like to leave Eden with its moods and hills. Each day has found our surroundings burning deeper and deeper into our memory. We can only say in leaving that we

[165]

are more sure of its friendship than of many friends. These hills will be faithful throughout the white silence. Parting with a woodland that one loves, with a hill-top that one cherishes, with a lake that one has been on, been in, and been across—such a farewell is the full-hearted choking farewell of a small child to a loved teacher. So we are, children in the school of the hills, from which we do not graduate, nor ever can; but which we leave for a recess.

How pleasant to think that those tall spruces on the point will be right there, barring exceptional weather, waiting for we prodigals, who will have wasted the strength they gave us.

Adiós

A GLIMPSE OF A MAN

Man and his world. From theologian to psychiatrist this relationship has sired countless books, fostered endless essays, many of them quickly forgotten. When once man could with impunity study, analyze, and challenge fundamental and established dogma, once man could brave the scorn of inquisitions, he tried to find the nature of the world and meaning of his all too brief passage through it. His searchings have always been far more certain than his findings or his conclusions. It has, however, always been the search that was important. From Socrates to Joshua Loth Liebmann the eagerness has been the same; the restless, ubiquitous, inquiring spirit.

Ten years ago a New Englander traveling in the fragrant islands of the Trade Winds paused a while in the Cook and Society Groups. There, as in other lands he had visited, he became impressed that it was the singer of the people who won and maintained the highest respect. The songs survived the forgotten deeds of the strong men. It was the poet of Polynesia who had the knowledge of the old meanings. Though often unwritten, he knew the old beliefs that made life good and proper to his fellows. They chanted his lore to the insistent beat of the *pohu* drums. The themes were all of the land and sea and men about them. It seems natural to the observer that these stalwart sentimental South Sea Islanders should take their inspiration from the natural characteristics of their island: its reefs and the rugged steeply rising mountains, with hurried streams. Their deep interest in each other was a light-hearted analysis of laughter, a childlike sympathy with tears, even anger, but totally different from the superficial frenzy of attention which civilization calls gossip. This was well summed up by the head of the Cook Island Maoris, the profoundly respected and fatherly patriarch, the venerable Makea Ea. Sitting thoughtfully on the porch of his *whare* he told the American what was, for the Polynesian, the true way to live fully and richly. His formula stated that the deepest duty and greatest beauty was for man to become attuned to his surrounding world, a simple matter, devoid of introversion and its complications. The process required that man be a great listener, completely attentive to everything about him. He was to be a warm lover, as he in turn was the beloved of his gods in nature. The ritual was slight and seasonal, and the rhetoric was supplied by wind, wave, and palm tree. No formalistic teaching but the passion, hate, love, and longing in the songs of the leading chanter made the men conscious of their folk-spirit.

In this last decade, nay, in this whole last generation all types of political and social trials and terrors have been perpetrated all over this earth and especially in its supposedly more enlightened parts, in the name of *the people*. A new Baal has arisen multimouthed and always surly, called the proletariat. Never before have phrases been so promiscuously and mischievously bandied about, such as: "the people's century, the voice of the people, the age of the common man, the age of the workers" (never to mean the age of the craftsman). Such all-inclusive phrases have always been applied to social leverage, and in no way to a natural relationship as envisioned in the philosophy of the Polynesian father. In fact, each such phrase has carried a corollary of violence and disruption rather than a sensitive and tolerant communion, seasoned by gentle good humor. And so in this day and in this Western world of more self-conscious

[168]

civilization we wonder where the voice of *the people* really does exist. In political and economic spheres the voice is halt and incomplete. There is the hunger, aspiration, greed, power of the masses, but never their dream, the fond hope, the heart of each; for in the truest measure *the people* is always but the massing of that inviolable quantity *the person*.

If the folk song is the place for this personal inner life, both lyric and tragic, where and how does the folksinger gain his voice? Robert Burns, lusty ploughman of Ayr, gives us, for Scotland, the answer. Brief was his attention to politics, small his dalliance on dogma, but wide and compassionate and heedful was his approach to the loves and sorrows of his fellow man, his kindred earth and its little creatures. Most truly he fulfilled the requirements for being the voice of his people. There is no time limit to such a voice. In Natal, New Zealand, New York or Calgary, Scotsmen can today become misty-eyed as their Bobby's songs are chanted to them. He speaks to them not as to something in their actual personal experience, but of something deep and enduring in their race pattern, something atavistic and eternal in their hearts.

In Spain it had long been hard to find a François Villon or a Robert Burns. The coercive zeal of religion and the rigid religious control of what should be printed has tended to prune away the earthy, the profane and the natural themes. The gypsy *cante hondo* of Granada and the surrounding countryside had a popular appeal and there was later even something slightly folklorish in the oddments of song in the *zarzuela,* a light sort of musical comedy. It was an appeal in the line of entertainment, but it had no deep resources of feeling in which the man and woman of the village and field could find themselves.

Federico García Lorca was born in the rich countryside of Granada at the end of the nineteenth century, the son of self-respecting Andalusian farmers, residing in the parochial village of Fuentevaqueros (The Fountain of the Herdsmen). Nearby were the shadowy deep ravines of the Moorish legends. Here was properly born the first fully uncensored voice of the people. His life of so short a span was lived intensively in the whole experience of being a Spanish man with all his conflicts of character and passion. He was a Spaniard as much of the 10th Century as he was of the 20th century, perhaps more so. He felt, probably far better than he would have been able to identify genealogically, his Moorish blood. He easily saw himself as one who rode with the *alguaciles* on their Arab mounts brought from the far Caliphate, to assail those dusty eroded hills of crumbling rocks rising above the great plain . . . the *vega* . . . of Granada, wide, green, and brown, rimmed with olive trees. The hills were tufted with fumbling cork trees and tumbled powdery fortresses.

Lorca traveled often to Madrid and even to the outside un-Spanish world of Paris and New York, but always it was to return to his gypsies, his Granada, for he was first and finally an Andalusian and secondly a Spaniard. Completely receptive to the whole of rural and village life about him, he was early popular as the story-teller and fancifier of his playmates. Equally early he was suspicious, then rebellious, against the unaltering religious and social patterns which formed doctrinal hedges around his villages. He found politics loathsome and insincere. In the last years of his life violent political forces tried to identify him as their spokesman, a "one-of-us" assumption which he rejected. Never did he forgive the Barcelona theatrical company that produced one of his plays for political propaganda.[1] When

[1]Apparently Cummings refers to the production of *Doña Rosita la Soltera.*

his alert compassion and consciousness of injustice might easily have turned him into social programs, the violences inherent in the pattern and in all akin to it made him at once reject the socialist platform. Politically he could only be called an individualist, if such there is, politically speaking.

Lorca had but two dimensions in all his thinking and writing: the *pueblo* . . . the village (even if it were a ward in a city) and the man, especially the anonymous little man. It was precisely for this inarticulate little man that he became the spokesman. His continuous barbed thrusts at the County Constabulary—the *Guardia Civil*—was his remonstrance for the villager against these unflinching arms of the law ceaselessly patrolling country lanes and mountain passes.

Another dominant quality in any man who serves as the voice of his countrymen must be his ability to accept and immerse himself into the superstitions and symbolisms of the village folk: into tradition, legend, folk history and the local supernatural. In no part of Europe is there more legend and tale, fear and nether-worldliness, than in the Moorish frontiers of Andalusia. Washington Irving sensed this and wrote of it as an onlooker who could not be partaker. Just as Robert Burns needs interpretation for the non-Celt, so does Lorca require much explanation to the reader (of his own tongue as well as in translation) in any other country, and even in his cousinly Gallicia and Cataluña. In each of these men, explanations often fall short of clarification, for the innate pattern of a people can only be fully comprehended by that folk. It is its identifying ethos. This is usually disaster for the translator.

It was a hot July afternoon when the writer first met Federico García Lorca at the Residencia de Estudiantes in Calle Pinar, 21, in Madrid. It was siesta period, and a New Englander under fifty never gives himself easily to the

[171]

pattern of afternoon naps. In the shadowy recreation hall someone was playing strong minor melancholy melodies . . . and note the word strong, for there is no whining weakness in the melancholy lament of the Andalusian. It was Lorca. All his life he collected the old songs of the gypsy and villager of Andalusia. He knew the Christmas carols half a millenium nearer Christ than ours. He was a searcher for the medieval music when the Arab influence was a living thing. Of all this collection of his, there remain only the resultant cadences and nuances in his poems, in their original words, and a few recordings with the folk dancer and singer, La Argentinita. He was tolerant of the wonder of the American and kindly in his explanations; then they both found they were countryfolk, and friendship stemmed from that. Down beyond the Rastro or public market where the strangest oddments of the most questionable origin were sold, there were cafés of muleteers and market gardeners, and in these together the young men found a quality not known in the Plaza Mayor or the Puerta del Sol.

Federico was a familiar of the National Theatre, the Teatro Español with Margarita Xirgu as its shining light. She and her company are now dispersed over the whole earth. They put on experimental plays and those included works of Federico. It was an oasis of comprehension in the capital. Federico particularly loathed the group of dilettantes who tried to make him fashionable. He once said that he met and kindled eager minds, but that over half of them turned from creative dreams to politics, that special mania of the young men, his contemporaries, in the Spain of the 1920's and 1930's.

Some of his family survive and they are more visibly proud of their relationship than they were, perhaps, in his lifetime. Life with a genius is often more palatable in retrospect. His frank denunciations of convention and

[172]

parochial edicts were embarrassing to all who wished to live unmolested. He did not marry, but in a larger sense Andalusia was his family and in every home, at every threshold, he was partaker of the common bread, common agony, common earthy laughter of the villager and the herdsman. He might even be said to have had too cosmic a sense of his relation to his villagers ever to have been a home-maker himself. He was a sort of Spanish Johnny Appleseed striding into the village, enriching the countryside and then striding off over some ancient horizon, spreading not apple seeds but songs, and gathering the hurts and happinesses of his people. Strange, then, it is that for all his wide sense of his human family he found in the minutiae of nature his best symbols: the tiniest leaf might be the burden-bearer of a resounding philosophy, or a feather the token of an ancient lost love. He sang of the lost greatness of his people, not in mourning a lost Armada but in all the lost years when the people were voiceless and their creativeness went unused. He was a man both sad and lonely, not because he was antisocial but because he longed for all the men who had ever been in Andalusia and for all the ages which would come to be familiar with that earth, and for the common people of all the earth in their shops, ships, and villages.

When in the summer of 1929 Federico García Lorca came under the auspices of a Guggenheim Fellowship to America[2] and more specifically to Columbia University, he renewed the friendship started in the siesta hour of that hot July of some years before.[3] He was homesick for Spain before he left Europe and he was hungry, as he said, for all

[2]I have been unable to confirm that Lorca received any aid from the Guggenheim Foundation; he is not in their published list of Fellows.

[3]Of 1928.

its beloved imperfections, all the time he was away from it.

At that time the writer was a much younger, much wordier, and more daring man. He wrote a journal of those days when in the month of August these countrymen were again in the rural villages and pastures. It is a most honest if naive and nostalgic journal. It could be rewritten with hindsight and a measure of maturity but it is this nostalgic quality that makes it most perfectly encase its subject. It records Federico García Lorca in the matrix of the Vermont high ridge country. Here again he became attuned to nature. He felt at home even though unable to communicate with the villagers about him, or with the writer's mother. It is possible to still see him giving a morning's flattering attention to her making doughnuts, whose name he never mastered. Eden Lake is a lost little lake in the books of lure to the Green Mountains, but it was there and on the hills that surround it that Federico García Lorca enjoyed the folk life of another people.

Each man has his golden age of indiscretion and immaturity and perhaps he can identify himself in this record written as it happened, when Eden seemed a lot nearer than it does when a man is twenty years older.

THE MIND OF GENIUS

Throughout any contact with the works of Federico García Lorca, as in any contact with the poet himself, there was the constant feeling that here was a thought-process unlike any other. In writing of the poet's life he was easily, in fact too easily, summed up as a genius. That may cover a multitude of evils and blessings from the utter neurotic to the eminently sublime. Let us try to unravel the fibres of this genius in the manner of thought. The Germans often speak of the very basic and very ancient ideas as coming from the *Ursprung,* the ultimate source, the ancient of days. In Lorca there was much that was as Spanish as Andalusia, as Arabic as Boabdil, and as Iberian as the famed Dama de Elche. His feeling for the past was not in the field of genealogy. He cared little for the past of his immediate family but was concerned with the entire roots of the people, the *pueblo.* Genius seems to me to be perhaps defined in one of its best facets in the possession of a consciousness of the soul of a people. And who shall say that one who has compassion for the soul of a race has not also the sense of the Universal Soul?

So often the poet Lorca has been stigmatized by the unsympathetic public, both native and alien, as a re-volutionary. Rejected in the political sense, it is entirely true of his imagination. He was in open rebellion against three things, all of them traditionally present in the Spain of Lorca's lifetime.

First and foremost Federico had a deep sense of justice for the people. That does not mean that he made a fetish of persons, for he saw them as composite. In all his poetry his named persons are symbols of the whole group, social stratum, or common experience. He hated injustice, and in this hating he made many individual observations as the personification of a whole situation. In his *Lament for Ignacio Sánchez Mejías,* the bullfighter, Lorca fought the blind flight of rejection of age and its inevitable changes in man. Lorca knew Mejías and was bound to feel his death, from an unwise return to the bullring after retirement, as a personal loss of great magnitude. Yet typical of Lorca, he wrote of this as the nostalgic mourning for youth gone, gone, gone. There was about Federico García Lorca a fierce love of life, a deep love of his friends, deeper than most people dare to feel, and a bitter rejection of the erosion of years on man and on his loves. In more than one place Lorca writes of the bitter injustice of Death itself, even though a relief from the life that was, yet never the answer to the life that might have been. In that dawn of his death, I dare believe that Lorca had a flashing sense that this bitter injustice conquers all, even his own life and his own unsung songs. In his strong love of life he was not only concerned with the physical, for which he had a deep appreciation, but for the honest singing soul.

Lorca hated most of all tangible evidences of the loss of man's freedom, the County Police called the *Guardia Civiles,* who in relentless pairs, in their hard black oilcloth hats, strode the dusty highways and byways of all Spain. As police they had a good record for bringing in the criminal, but as agents of coercion enforcing the small laws of local *alcaldes* and other functionaries, they were as inescapable as the seasons. Like sombre pendulums they moved across the face of Spain and the people cringed in fear and hopelessness. Back and forth these unsmiling pairs strolled the roads and paths, and their movements, dark as night, were symbols of arrogance and death. In no poem does he become more caustic than in his "Romance de la Guardia Civil española." Here are two strophes of his poem in which burn all the fierceness of the poet's reaction:

"Yet comes the Guardia Civil
Sowing flames on the way
Wherein the young and
Honest imagination are consumed."

. . .

"Oh, City of the Gypsies
The Guardia Civil goes into the distance
Down a tunnel of silence
While the flames draw ever near you."

Wherever the Guardia Civil passed by, something died in the soul. The American policeman and the British constable never inspired this reaction in any save those troubled by their conscience. To Lorca the Guardia was the Stygian coldness that froze songs, killed dreams and bore about it the starkness of the misery of the poor and the immediacy of death. Blasco Ibáñez, in his *Four Horsemen of the Apocalypse,* similarly invested his symbols with this powerful allegory.

The third great hate was for the Roman Catholic tradition in which the freedoms of expression and action seemed to him so imprisoned and constrained. From many afternoons and long nights with him, I can say that he was a man of enormous Faith and deep Trust, but it was a Faith uncontained in any ritual lesser than the winds across the *vega* or

[177]

the storms astride the *sierra*. The confessional was to him anathema, in that he felt that a man could bare his soul and its weaknesses only in a great and companionable friendship, a free concept of total love and a condition of complete experience of body, heart, and mind. It may have been the very power of this censure which still keeps Lorca's books off the shelves of the safely devout, that conspired in those early days of the Spanish Revolution to destroy him. No power is more relentless in its pursuit of the iconoclast than an established and state Church. Into the lives of the very poor it reaches with peace and beauty in return for total submission to a code of ethics which seems to be fraught with fear and to give little hope for the searching of the dreamer or singer for his own mode of expression. It is in no way a commentary on the inviolable Sacraments of the Church to say that Federico rejected Catholicism because it bound him to follow laws of behavior and patterns of thinking which he considered unsuited to a man of self-respect. Even so, the whole of life was a sort of tremendous celebration of the Mass to Federico. For truly evident is the fact that while he rejected the formal Church he was a man of intense philosophy. I recall one evening when we were on the night express from Irún to Paris, as Federico was traveling with Don Fernando de los Ríos and his daughter, we shared a second-class compartment to ourselves. We stretched out and he talked for hours to the rhythmic click of the wheels over the rails, of what life was for and that man was always playing hide-and-seek with death. I asked him what the meaning of life really was to him. His reply was simple. "Felipe, life is laughter, amid a rosary of deaths; it is to look beyond the braying man to the love in the heart of the people. It is being the wind and ruffling the waters of a brook. It is coming from nowhere and going to nowhere and

[178]

being everywhere with many tears around you." I believe that can be read to mean a strong love of life. It was a Greek philosopher who said "the great lover of life is the beloved of the Gods." As was natural, Federico in all his writings, poetic and dramatic, found himself against the dicta of the Church. At times I suspect he chose certain broad similes to confound the stolidly conventional. As his posthumous fame grows Lorca will probably come to be accepted by this group but they will have to do some tall interpretations of his poetry to make it fit their admissable scheme of things, and I fancy I can almost hear Federico's laughter. One day he told me at the Residencia de Estudiantes he was going on a long walk. I asked him the reason and he replied "To find the heart of a little man in some stuffed shirts."

Through the whole of Federico García Lorca's genius this way of facing life, these resentments and the moments of deepest pain as well as moments of nonsense (and these were not too many) were his constant thought patterns. Probably few men have ever seen so many things as always symbols of peoples, patterns, and moods. When he walked with you in his sacred city of Granada you felt that you had an invitation to tea at the Alhambra with Boabdil waiting in the Court of Lions, for he had built for you the whole of the Arabic capital. To go to the caves of the Gypsies was to become a member of their ancient band so long as Federico was there. He was at home in the desperate lunges and stout stampings of the flamencos and the *cante jondos*. Walking in Madrid on a clammy late autumn day of rain, Federico expanded in deep thoughts and one statement remains sharply with me: "*Oiga*, Felipe, this rain comes chattering out of the mountains, shivering with the cold. It came from the Escorial where all the cold dead rains are born." We were on our way to a rehearsal of Margarita Xirgu at the Teatro

[179]

Español. That whole walk he was in a mood of "translation" of the visible into the intangible. A similar walk in the forests of Mount Norris in Vermont was in just this key. When Federico was in his mood of tenseness he fastened heroic symbols onto the least of things.

There was also a lyric Lorca who carved images as lacy as the most choice of Arabic filigree.

> "Below the image of Moses
> The incense went to sleep."
>
>   ("La soltera en misa")

> "The night sings naked
> As she crosses the rivers of March."
>
>   ("Serenata")

> "The day fades slowly
> Bearing the long afternoon over its shoulder."
>
>   ("Prendimiento
>   de Antoñito el
>   Camborio")

In speaking of a reflection in the water he wrote: "The flower went wavering down the stairway of water."

Who shall say that man does not live more richly in this fashion of seeing all in its related aspects? More than meets the eye, more than reaches the ear or nostril; these overtones were for Lorca the meshes in a strainer through which he was forever pouring life.

His manner of stating was as startling as his manner of seeing. He made his most telling similes in a few words, searing in their combinations yet basically simple little words. He has not left us a vast bulk of works, yet in those poems, dramas, and occasional articles or lectures stands the heritage of Iberia, Granada, and Spain, traced indelibly, positively and pungently with a fierce freedom. His was a genius unfettered, bold and compassionate. He who finds Lorca enigmatic is like so many of us, uncomfortable before stark truths, relentlessly presented and daringly pursued.

THE POEMS

Federico was not a prolific writer, but there are probably scores of unedited and unpublished poems. His literary remains are probably mostly in the hands of his friend, the poet Bergamín. There were manuscript poems in the hands of his great friend and fellow-lover of all that was Spanish, the late Manuel de Falla.[1] The contemporary poet Rafael Alberti may have a few.

His books were *Libro de poemas*, 1921, *Canciones (Songs)*, 1927, the widely known *Romancero gitano*, 1928, which has been called the most remarkable best-seller in Spanish poetic literature. There is a posthumous collection *Poet in New York (Poeta en Nueva York)*, with a prologue by his literary executor, José Bergamín. His plays are headed by the rural tragedy, *Nuptials in Blood (Bodas de sangre)*. *Yerma* followed and then *Doña Rosita la soltera (Miss Rose, Spinster)*.

When Federico García Lorca was in the writer's cottage at Lake Eden, Vermont, there were long discussions on words and their visible and invisible meanings. This may have been his period of preparation for what is called his surrealist poetry, which appeared toward the end of his life. The New Englander accepted his challenge and translated the book *Canciones (Canciones, 1921–1924, Segunda Edición, Revista de Occidente, Madrid 1929)*. Each poem was a mental wrestling match. The translations stand as approved by

---

[1]There is reason to believe that Bergamín has manuscripts of *El público*, the *Sonetos de amor oscuro,* and the missing manuscript of *Poeta en Nueva York.* (See my *Textual Tradition.*) If Falla had manuscripts of Lorca, they have never been recovered.

[183]

Federico. These "approved" translations might be bettered today but here they stand inviolate. The choice has been limited to those most easily understood in the experience of reasonably curious American readers.[2]

A new translation of selected poems was published in America late in 1947 by the Transatlantic Arts Inc. and printed by The Hogarth Press in London (Lund, Humphries, London and Bradford). This small volume is the excellent translation by J. L. Gili and Stephen Spender. For one who has facility in reading Spanish the prologue "Federico García Lorca (La muerte vencida)" by José Bergamín is an important contribution. It appears in the volume *Poeta en Nueva York* por Federico García Lorca, published by the Editorial Séneca, México D.F. 1940. One day when Spain may again breathe free air, Lorca's poems will again be published in his own land where his blood flowed from violence into the soil of Granada.

[2]The entire book is included in this edition.